Published &
edited by

viction:ary™

Uncover the
power of graphics
in fashion

First published and distributed by
viction:workshop ltd.

viction:ary™

Unit C, 7th Floor, Seabright Plaza,
9-23 Shell Street, North Point Hong Kong
URL: www.victionary.com
Email: we@victionary.com

Edited and produced by viction:workshop ltd.
Preface by Ada Yan Tsuen Fung

Book design by viction:design workshop
Concepts & art direction by Victor Cheung
Cover illustration by Kustaa Saksi (Unit CMA)

Cover printed on Sun Printable Cloth - Cot White
165gsm, sponsored by Acumen Paper Limited.

ISBN 978-988-98228-8-0

Printed and bound in China

Key to symbols:

 Apparel  Accessories  Prints  Display

Content

Graphic design is interwoven into the fabric of fashion. At a time when exclusivity is the holy-grail in fashion, graphic design provides the means to pinpoint, differentiate and communicate a unique identity. In fact, graphic design has become elemental with communications in all shapes and forms (real or virtual)that, it is not an accentuation to say that there will be no fashion to speak of without the language of graphic design.

Mentioning the influence of graphic design in fashion, the first thing that comes to one's mind is its vital role in branding. Combining ingenious creativity with calculated business awareness, a logo makes first (and lasting) impression. It identifies and promotes, as well as serving the purpose as a stamp of approval and therefore ensures exclusivity. The absence of a recognisable logo, however, is namely an anti-logo statement. Such statement, made by avant-garde companies such as Martin Margiela is just as conscious. The Comme des Garcon 'Play' quirky heart logo, created by artist Filip Pagowski, is a glorious example of how a logo can also embody an off-beat, not-so-commercial appeal. Of course one could argue that the absence of a logo is, in fact, a logo.

Fashion images are instrumental to all kinds of fashion communications and an important component to the machine named fashion industry. Fashion images conjure as much, if not more, allure of fashion. Tom Ford (the famous ex-creative director for Gucci) reportedly claimed that a flawlessly executed advertising campaign has the power to lift sales for a less-than-perfect collection. Fashion image is an extremely persuasive visual language- Think of Helmut Newton and his image of powerful female fatale; or Mario Sorrenti and his sensual, iconic black and white images of Kate Moss for Calvin Klein. Images construct a desired lifestyle that one wants to belong to. Mention the name of local hero Wing Shya and his atmospheric images for Wong Kar Wai films instantly spring to mind. His highly stylised images are evidential in many fashion projects Shya-La-La (his production company) is involved in. The polished fashion images triggers a back-lash of 'real' images started by iconic style magazines such as i-D and The Face in the Eighties. The effect is proved to be enduring and still widely evidential in fashion images related to contemporary avant-garde labels such as Material by Product. In which images seem to be taken as is, with minimal styling. Fashion image began life as illustration and started in the 16th Century. However, fashion illustration is by no means done and dusted. Instead it is celebrated as a caliber of work in its own right, thanks to a new wave of illustrators such as Julie Verhoeven. She has (arguably) single-handedly resurrect authentic, hand-drawn illustration. Other recent alumni includes Deanne Cheuk, whose watercolour-based illustration for the New York-based style magazine Tokion has earned her a cult following. However, highly polished looking computer-art illustration, such as the ones by Catalina Estrada, reminds one it is in fact a digital age we are living in.

Both employ typography, image and logo, one could argue that advertising is recognised as a hard-sell tool as opposed to fashion editorial. But just to give you an idea, there are four hundreds images in average in every issue of Vogue, each carefully chosen to articulate a coherent message. The rise of 'Art Director', such as Fabien Baron in US and Peter Saville in UK are instrumental to the integration of fashion and graphics. Both are influential figures of fashion image maker, their keen eyes on graphics brought a fresh perspective in fashion editorial and advertising. Consider the fact that art directors and graphic designers have always produced advertising campaigns as well as editorial, the line between the two is blurred. In fact, the two are quite rightly described as different sides of the same coin. It is important to note that advertising is not just a high-end fashion phenomenon. The high street retailer Marks & Spencer claimed that their recent fashion campaign featuring Sixties fashion icons Twiggy successfully drew nineteen million customers to their nation-wide stores last year. Saturday, the London-based design agency, produces effective advertising campaigns for avant-garde brands such as Preen as well as the classic stationer Smythson. Fashion promotion does not just stop there. Press-releases, look books and invitations, which are aimed at the (mostly jaded) journalists, can definitely claim to be an art in its own right. Base Design, who counts Chloe, Superfine and L'oreal as clients, certainly knows how.

The boom of the internet in the Nouties has revolutionised marketing in all aspects. Internet marketing is lower in cost, faster in pace and reaches out to a much wider customer base. Website simply becomes an essential marketing tool to any fashion businesses who worth their salt. Fashion websites and blogs provide new means to access trends and one can even see fashion shows real time with just a click of a but-

ton. More importantly, online shopping has transformed the model of consumption and is the perfect medium for the disposable mode of 'fast-fashion' consumption. MySpace, a non-fashion orientated website, was responsible for directing twelve percent of Top Shop's customers to its website in 2006. Avant-garde website such as SHOWstudio takes advantage of the technology and pushes the boundaries of image making by involving viewers in a degree that is unheard of previously.

There was a time when print was tired and very much worn by rich middle-aged housewives only, but it is long-gone. Following the revamp of print- heavy fashion houses such as Cacharel, Pucci and Missoni (whose last show was styled by none other than Nicola Formechetti, the art director of Dazed & Confused), print has been injected with a new charm and features heavily in many young designers. Jonathan Saunders is recognised by his body conscious, rainbow palette prints in his collections; Giles Deacon created bold prints inspired by American artist Ellsworth Kelly for his A/W 06 collection; Basso & Brooke wowed the London fashion scene with their censor-worthy but fairy-tale like prints and subsequently won the first ever Fashion Fringe competition in 2005. On the other hand, clean and girly fashion prints in the style of Bob Foundation and Eley Kishimoto and the others provide a retro yet modern alternative. Graphic design is also evidential in fashion accessories. Big, bold and statement-making accessories (like Tatty Devine and the others) have crawled their way from street fashion to grace the pages of the likes of Vogue and i-D.

After logo-mania in the Eighties and political slogans in the Nineties, t-shirts are adopted as uniform of Hip Hop crowd. The focus shifted from a strong message to the loose fit and a some-what non-statement. Of course, t-shirt is such a timeless and functional item of clothing that can resist any fashion trends. Curiously, House of Holland by Henry Holland has recently resurrected slogan t-shirts with ironic fashion victim messages.

Set design, like the name suggests, sets the stage for fashion fantasies. It is essential for editorial fashion shoots, advertising campaigns and retail spaces. It channels a capsule fashion universe that is made of dreams and gives the viewer to a physical experience to remember. It can be a room, a smell and a sound that add up to an atmosphere that envelops and thrills. On designing a space for Calvin Klein A/W 07 collection presentation, Japanese architect Shinichi

Ogawa commented that 'fashion and architecture are both things that envelop people.' Alexander McQueen's fashion shows in his early years were famous for guaranteed spectacle and controversy such as run down gothic merry-go-round, fanciful Twenties-que dance floor, Gigantic glass box that exploded at finale and 'golden shower' that sprays to the privileged viewers on front row. Another lover of such spectacle is Victor & Rolf and their shows are simply mesmerizing - blue screens with pattern projected onto clothes, poles with spotlight that hang oversize lapels or arms of clothing off the models; layers of outfit, shied one by one during the show, doubled as the set design. Newcomer Herik Vibskov (whose work you will see in the following chapter) demonstrates how an immaculately executed set can transform a square room into an otherworldly delight. Roomful of matt black carrot suspended above a florescent yellow floor against the dark, or a field of gleaming silver figurines on broken eggshells under blinding strong light is surely not your average, everyday experience. Despite of the staggering costs to produce, the drama and energy catwalk shows can generate make them a press tool that is still second to none.

Retail space, focuses on its aesthetics and marketability, aims to push customers towards purchases in the most seductive, sensual way. From its lighting, visual merchandising to window display, every single aspect of presentation is calculated down to how the hem of the dress is draped on the mannequin. Graphic display such as futuristic streamlined interior in Marni shops creates an instant impact and communicates the identity of the company. Surface to Air's poetically eclectic aesthetic is displayed in 3-D form in the shape of their own store in Paris and the space they created for Dover Street Market in London. Selfridges Birmingham (UK) by Future System is also a prime example of how architecture can be utilised in the context of fashion.

Fashion Unfolding aims to document an on-going development between fashion and graphic design. As the two weave into each other, the face of fashion continues to be manifested in a manner that is as multi-faceted as ever. Bigger, better, more, in every sense. We believe it is a process that will change the landscape of fashion, graphic design and media as we know it.

Forest, a colour representative of the nature, signifies dreamlike quality of fairytales and otherworldly fantasies. It belongs to a heavenly place where the prince and princess live happily ever after, where everything is vivid and beautifully ornamented. This section demonstrates how colour can bring a poetic story into life.

FOREST

potipoti Graphic Fashion

Berlin, Germany

Title: Fábula Collection Fall/Winter 06/07 Designer: Nando & Silvia Photographer: Nacho Alegre Client: potipoti Graphic Fashion Description: To protect ourselves from the loneliness, as well as the cold, in the winter's long night, potipoti bring us a collection of popular fables made mohair, pure wool and other natural materials. Each garment is inspired in a different tale, using colours that evoke the mysterious nature where they take place, like black, brick red and oak wood brown.

potipoti Graphic Fashion

Berlin, Germany

Title: Fábula Collection Fall/Winter 06/07 Designer: Nando & Silvia Photographer: Nacho Alegre Client: potipoti Graphic Fashion Description: To protect ourselves from the loneliness, as well as the cold, in the winter's long night, potipoti bring us a collection of popular fables made mohair, pure wool and other natural materials. Each garment is inspired in a different tale, using colours that evoke the mysterious nature where they take place, like black, brick red and oak wood brown.

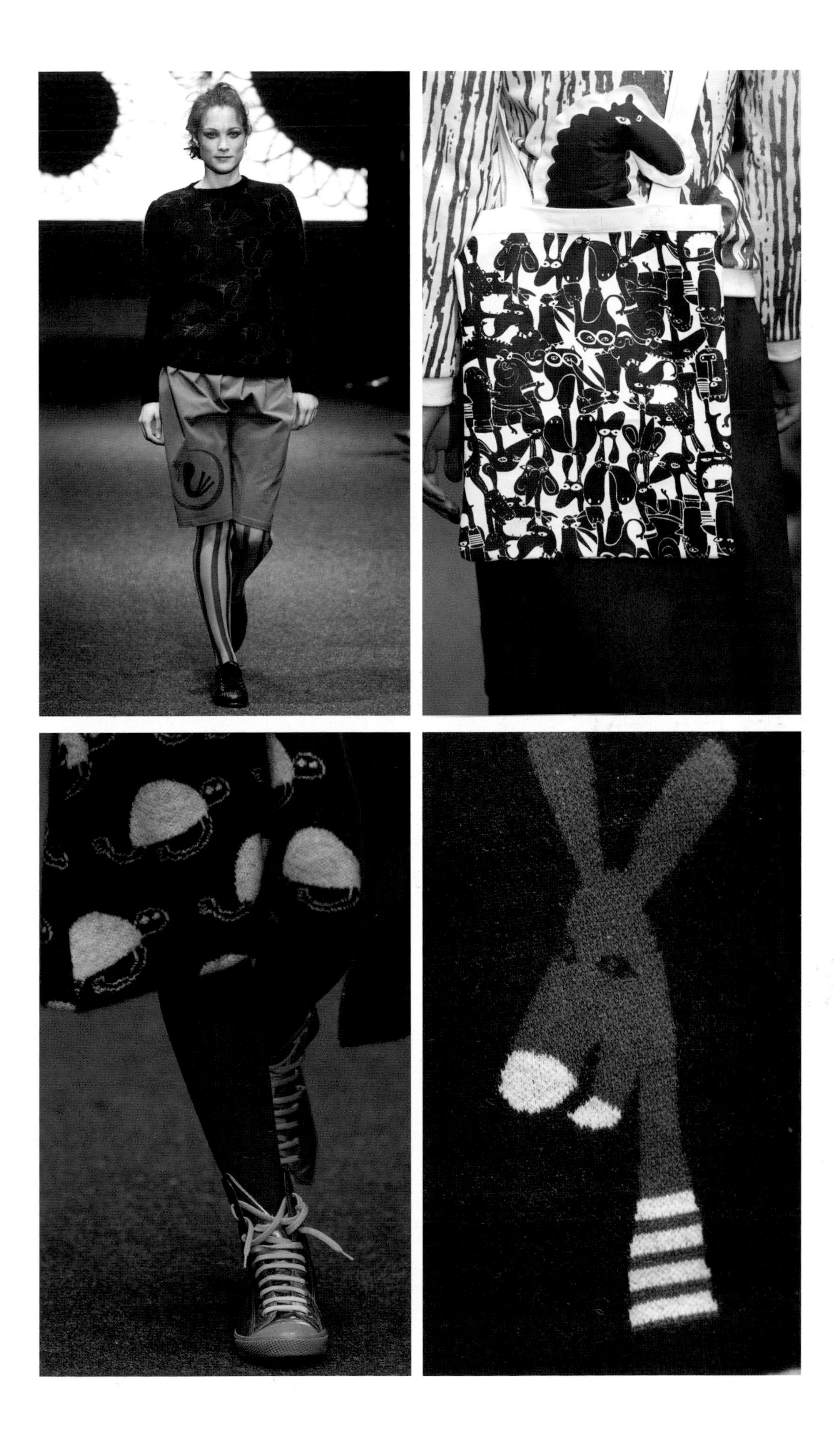

CROSSING WONDERLAND
And A + Bob Foundation

Tokyo, Japan

Title: CROSSING WONDERLAND
Designer: Hiromi Suzuki Client: And A Inc. Description: An idea of the project 'CROSSING WONDERLAND' is started with a story 'The Pied Piper of Hamelin' in which the man takes the children away with the sound of pipe. For the campaign of And A, the shop is set as a wonderland and the clowns lead visitors as if strange animals are welcoming to the wonderland. In the wonderland, the inhabitants are making the strange animal shadow pictures and the balloon animals. The visitors could also go through the process of making the wonderland.

Studio I'm JAC

Rotterdam, The Netherlands

* Title: honor revenge ** Title: matchgirl

*** Title: mother **** Title: eve

Designer: Irene Jacobs Client: JF&W Magazine

Description: 3 spreads for Jewels Fashion & Watches Magazine Spring 2006 - the designer had complete freedom to make illustrations in which the jewels of the advertisers had to be shown. She was inspired by Flemish paintings from around the fifteenth century like a painting from Jean Fouguet; La Vierge et l'enfant Jésus. She wanted to illustrate things in life that are as everlasting as jewels can be, like fear, love, seduction, power, hope and vulnerability.

The honor revenge illustration was developed for BLVD magazine, to go with an article About Honor revenge, it was never published in that magazine because they thought it was too harsh for the readers.

*

**

***

****

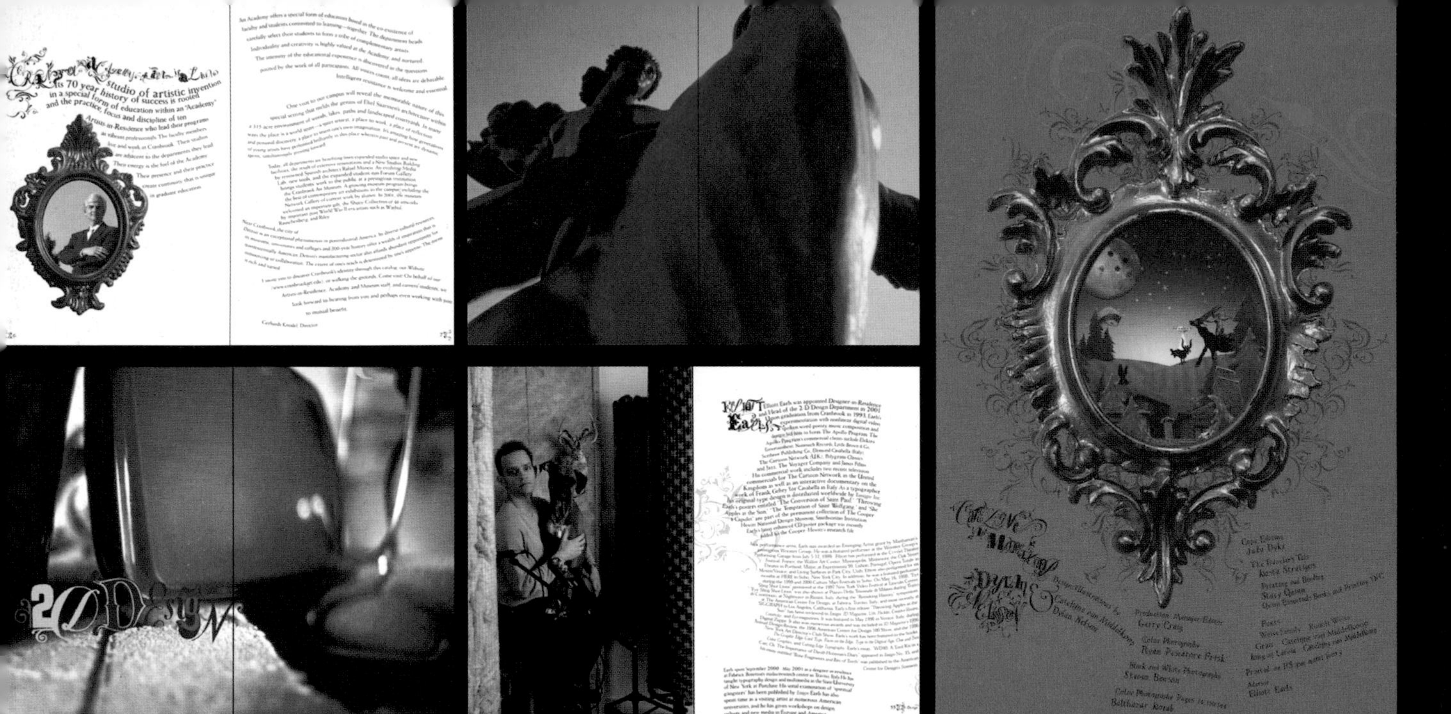

Oregon, USA

Title: - Designer: Dylan Nelson, Catelijne van Middelkoop Client: Cranbrook Academy of Art Description: Driven from the experiences at Cranbrook, Incubate teamed up with Strange Attractors to create the New Student Admissions Catalogue. Dubbed as 'The little red boo,' Incubate reinterpreted the idea of a traditional catalogue by creating a 256 paged, hard cover, foil stamped book, based on the mysterious, whimsical world that is Cranbrook Academy of Art.

(Next page) Title: - Designer: Dylan Nelson, Brian Acevedo Client: Saatchi + Saatchi : Foldgers Coffee Description: Saatchi + Saatchi asked Incubate to illustrate a surreal dream for Folgers Coffee - Tolerate Mornings Ad Campaign.

ARMY

Home
GUEST
DOWN
TO GO
BALL ON
PONG
CHAMP
GO TEAM

PAUL
SMITH

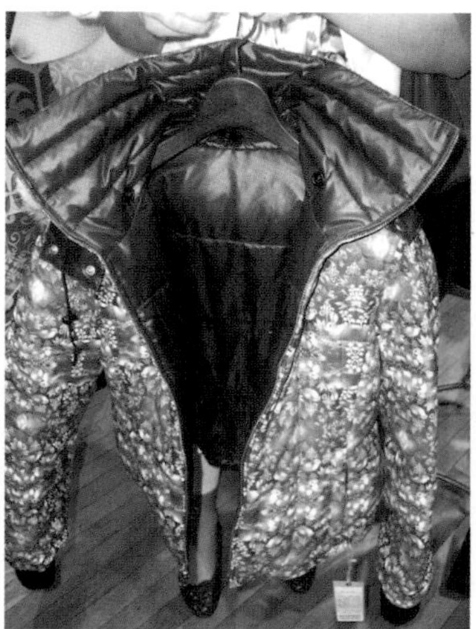

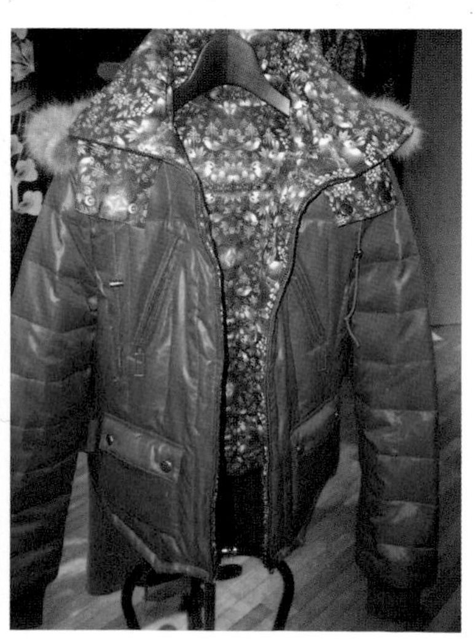

Catalina Estrada ★

Barcelona, Spain

Title: Animals in a London Park
Designer: Paul Smith Team Client: Paul Smith Description: The illustrations were created exclusively for the Paul Smith AW/07 collection. The brief was to create images of typical scenes and animals that you would find in a London Park. Each garment designed with these illustrations would have a label tag reading 'Catalina Estrada for Paul Smith.'

Catalina Estrada

Barcelona, Spain

Title: Animals in a London Park Designer: Paul Smith Team Client: Paul Smith Description: The illustrations were created exclusively for the Paul Smith AW/07 collection. The brief was to create images of typical scenes and animals that you would find in a London Park. Each garment designed with these illustrations would have a label tag reading 'Catalina Estrada for Paul Smith.'

Catalina Estrada

Barcelona, Spain

Title: Animals in a London Park
Designer: Paul Smith Team Client: Paul Smith Description: The illustrations were created exclusively for the Paul Smith AW/07 collection. The brief was to create images of typical scenes and animals that you would find in a London Park. Each garment designed with these illustrations would have a label tag reading 'Catalina Estrada for Paul Smith.'

Catalina Estrada

Barcelona, Spain

Title: Animals in a London Park Designer: Paul Smith Team Client: Paul Smith Description: The illustrations were created exclusively for the Paul Smith AW/07 collection. The brief was to create images of typical scenes and animals that you would find in a London Park. Each garment designed with these illustrations would have a label tag reading 'Catalina Estrada for Paul Smith.'

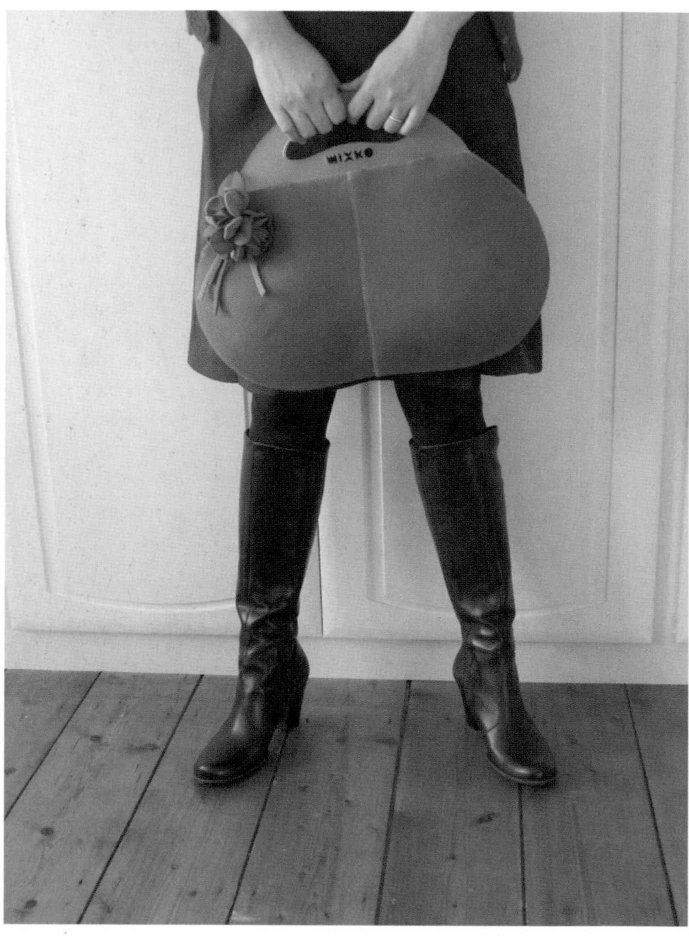

MIXKO

Devon, UK

Title: 'Clam' 2005 - Hat Trick Collection Client: - Designer: Nahoko Koyama Description: An equally modern and classic looking lady's handbag, decorated with a detachable corsage. Bag construction utilising 2 hat bodies. It's available in Antique Red, Poppy Red, Peacock and Light Beige.

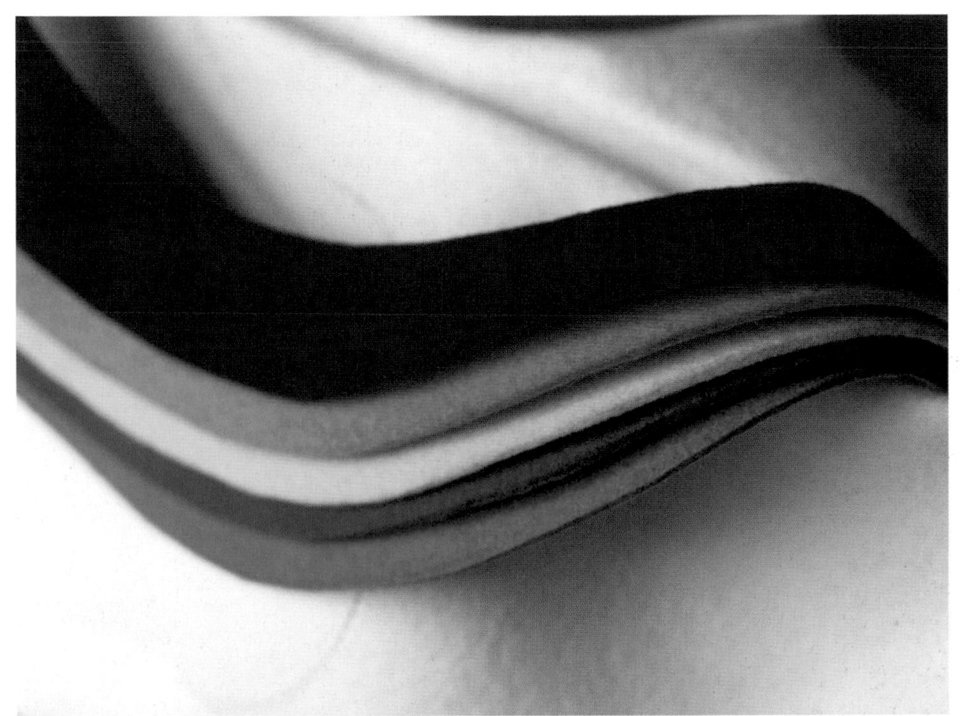

Devon, UK

Title: 'Rainbowbag' - Hat Trick Collection Client: - Designer: Nahoko Koyama Description: Same collection - this one's corsage is designed in rainbow colours.

Devon, UK

Title: 'Butterfly,''Stella,''Camellia' Rings, 2005 - Hat Trick Collection Client: - Designer: Nahoko Koyama Description: Decorative felt objects on clear acrylic rings. Produced entirely from off cuts.

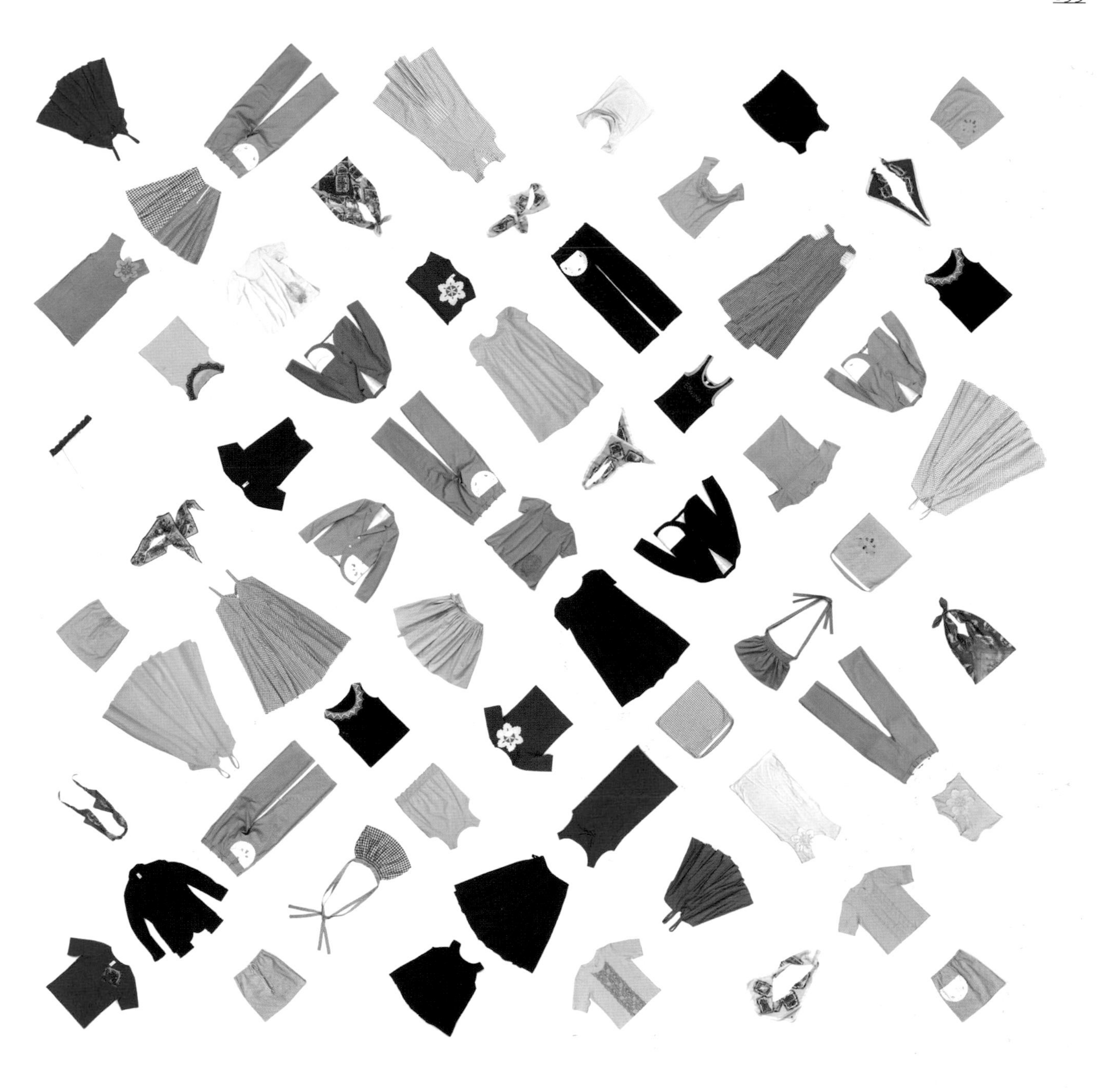

Edwina Hörl Japan

Tokyo, Japan

Title: edwina hörl nanikore (fashion catalog)
Client: edwina hörl Designer: Taku Anekawa
Description: Design and art direction by so+ba.

Kustaa Saksi (Unit CMA)

Paris, France

Title: A-POC Designer: Kustaa Saksi Client: Issey Miyake/A-POC Description: Promotion materials for anniversary of Issey Miyake's A-POC fashion line in Paris.

Stockholm, Sweden

Title: Spring/Summer 2005 Mask-sunglasses Designer: Johan Hjerpe Client: Diana Orving Description: An invitation for a cardboard mask with sun film. It is designed for a collection inspired by the thinking of female surrealists like Leonor Fini and Dorothea Tanning.

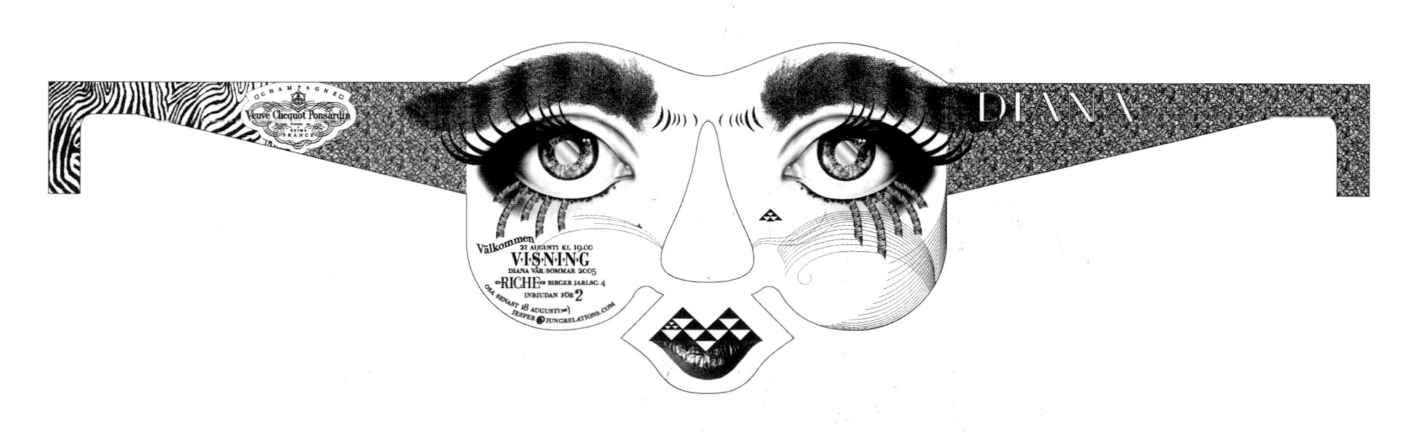

Gi Myao

London, UK

Title: Cat & Dog Badge Designer: Gi Myao Client: Two-B Fashion, London Description: Based on the 'Street Look' concept for Spring Summer 2005, this badge was created from a hand drawn 'Cat & Dog' icon illustration. Specially instructed to be silk embroidered by hand in order to keep the softness and details of the original drawing effect.

Making this badge look even more chic, fashionable and stand out, compared to other ordinary menswear badge designs.

This style of badge featured well with Two B's range of formal suits and casual sportswear collections.

TWO B

TWO B

TWO B

Kustaa Saksi (Unit CMA)

Paris, France

Title: Gentry Portofino Designer: Kustaa Saksi Photographer: Sune Czajkowski Client: Gentry Portofino Description: Classic Italian cashmere brand Gentry Portofino asked Saksi to make wallpaper designs and patterns to be used on their walls and fabrics, among Saksi's signature cashmere knitwear collection for Spring/Summer 2006. The colours of the wallpapers follow the same colour scale as the knitwear collection. The main theme is sea life - underwater views and imaginative characters. Giving fresh, maritime feeling mixing organic and inorganic shapes. Simplicity in the chaos. Bold shapes and contrasting colours.

Serial Cut™

Madrid, Spain

Title: WAD EUROPE Designer: idem Client: WAD Magazine (France) Description: Artwork for the French magazine, some still-life Photographer with cutout elements for the Northern Europe Special issue. For this special issue, WAD sent Serial Cut™ the images of the different models, which represent all the northern countries of Europe: Sweden, Norway, Denmark, Finland, Holland and Belgium. The usual still-life style of other works is also used in this project, but with a new element: splashes of real fresh paint, in different colours, representing each country's flag.

NOR
VEGE

Atomic Attack!

Hong Kong, China

Title: D-Mop Times Square Store opening campaign Designer: Calvin Ho Client: D-Mop Description: D-Mop is Hong Kong's leading and cutting edge fashion retail store. They needed a much younger audience appeal for its new Times Square opening since it was targeting more street casual wear and many new younger brands. Production time 5 days. The solution was to make it bright colourful and attractive with cool hip animals. Breakdancing rabbit, a sheep with individuality, and peacock showing its true colours.

OPEN
YOUR
MIND

OPEN
YOUR
MIND

ida
Bestseller By
IDA SJÖSTEDT
Ritz sweater
Sunny dress
Domino dress
Baby bikini
May dress
Lula top, Baby bikini bottoms
Twinkle top, Jazz sweaterdress
Jojo jumpsuit
Robin hood, Gigi tube
SALES & PRESS CONTACT: jus, + 46 8 611 98 00, www.idasjostedt.com. Photo: Kambiz/Söderberg Agentur, stylist: Angie, hair & make-up: Linda Sundqvist/Agent Bauer, model: Alice K/Stockholmsgruppen, prints & graphic design: Sara Hernández.

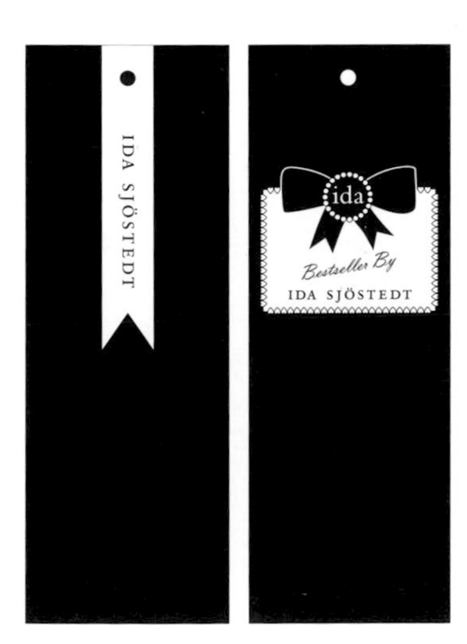

Sara Hernández

Sweden

Title: Ida Designer: Sara Hernández Client: Ida Sjöstedt (www.idasjostedt.com) Photographer: Kambiz Description: This spring 2007 Ida Sjöstedt introduces her sub label ida. A strong identity has developed. The logotype/symbol is built by graphic forms and constructed in a flexible way. It is made to be exposed on clothes like prints and patterns and in some prints only a part of it is used. Trompe lóeil prints in a strong graphic and pop-style touch gives an edge to the cute and streetsmart look. While for the sale & image catalogue for Ida Sjöstedt's collection 'Untitled' Autumn/Winter 2007, it is inspired by British Pantomimes. The designer staged a performance at a picturesque theatre where the models entertain, seduce and confuse playing the roles of princesses, pinups and variety girls. This was a collaboration project with art direction and design & illustration together with photographer Marcus Ohlsson and designer Ida Sjöstedt.

Something and Something Else

Sydney, Australia

Title: - Designer: Georgina Cullum Client: Fashion retailers Description: Various yardage textile prints designed for the Something Else Spring, Summer and Winter 07 collections.

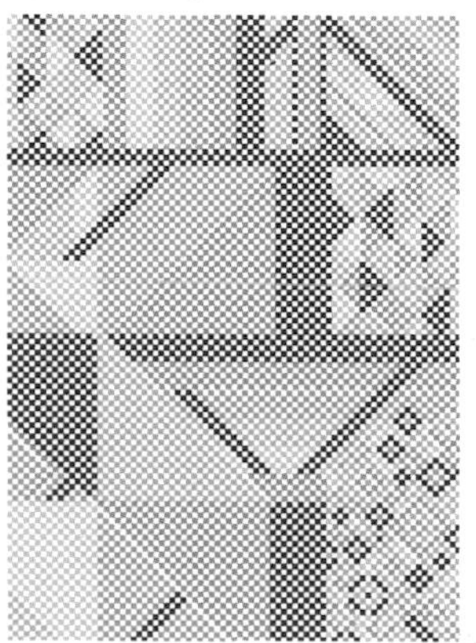

something

sôme
thing

SOMETHING ELSE

By Natalie Wood

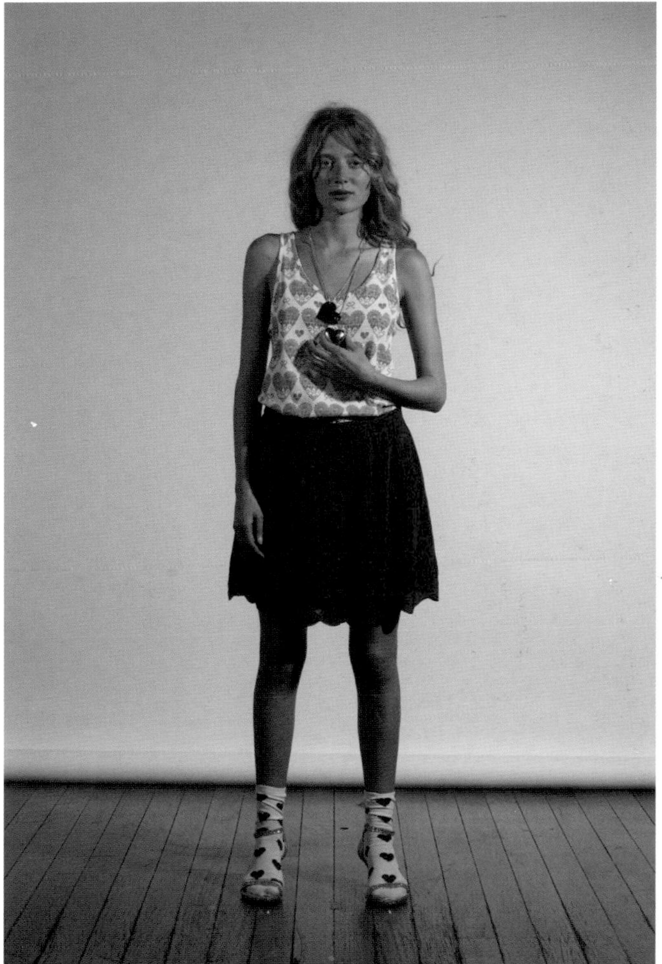

Deanne Cheuk Design
New York, USA

Title: EarthLiness Collection
Designer: Rilla Alexander, Deanne Cheuk, Yasmin Majidi Client: Liness
Description: An Earth obsessed collection for Liness, called EarthLiness. The poster also served as the lookbook for the collection. Each collection is based on a different obsession; previous collections were OwLiness, BoyLiness and SleepLiness. This collection featured designs including evolution, nature, and Mother Earth.

Something and Something Else

Sydney, Australia

Title: One Day I Stood Under a Very Large Tree Designer: Jonathan Zawada, Mary Libro Client: Fashion retailers and media Description: Promotional collectible book relating to the Autumn/Winter 07 Something Else collection.

TREES ABSORB ODOURS AND POLLUTANT GASES AND FILTER PARTICULATES OUT OF THE AIR TRAPPING THEM IN THEIR LEAVES AND BARK.
ONE ACRE OF TREES REMOVES 2.6 TONS OF CO2 A YEAR.

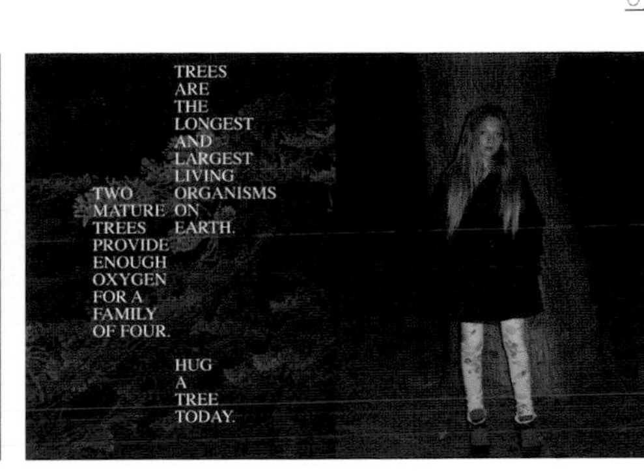
TREES ARE THE LONGEST AND LARGEST LIVING ORGANISMS ON EARTH.
TWO MATURE TREES PROVIDE ENOUGH OXYGEN FOR A FAMILY OF FOUR.
HUG A TREE TODAY.

CREATIVE DIRECTOR
NATALIE WOOD
PHOTOGRAPHER
PIERRE TOUSSAINT
STYLIST
DAVE BONNEY
HAIR
BRAD NGATA
MAKE UP
CLAIRE THOMPSON
MODEL
ZIPPORA VERMILLION ROSE SEVEN
SHOES
TRISTAN BLAIR
QUILT
VINTAGE CLOTHING SHOP
ART DIRECTION
MARY LIBRO
JONATHAN ZAWADA

27TH JULY 2007 NATIONAL TREE PLANTING DAY.
IF NOTHING ELSE TREES GIVE US AN EXCUSE TO SIT AND CLOSE OUR EYES AND LISTEN.

Shya-la-la Production Limited

Hong Kong, China

Title: Grabitti Designer: Sarah at Shyalala Client: Crossover A.T x Shyalala Description: Inspired by a 'Rabbit' character that is real, rock, retro to create an exciting range of fashion apparels and accessories titled 'Grabitti.'

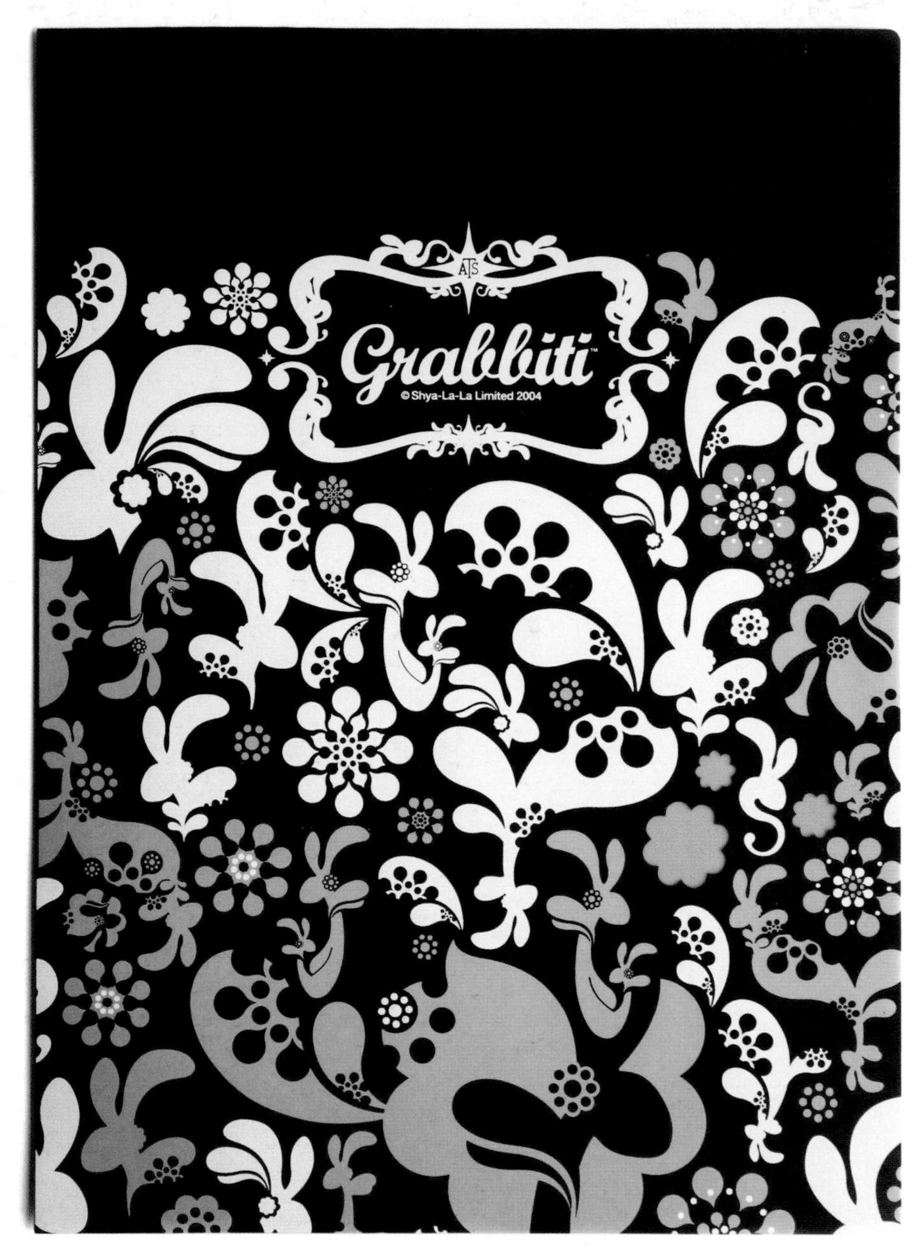

Shya-la-la
Production Limited

Hong Kong, China

Title: Grabitti Designer: Sarah at Shyalala Client: Crossover A.T x Shyalala Description: Inspired by a 'Rabbit' character that is real, rock, retro to create an exciting range of fashion apparels and accessories titled 'Grabitti.'

Fuchsia, a shocking hue of pink, always manages to capture one's attention. It serves as a fine metaphor for people who are energetic, dynamic and active – whose charm shine through in the crowd. In this section, the colour channels these characters and shows you how this quality is shared in a variety of work.

FUCHSIA

why not associates
London, UK

Title: Nike Paris Designer: why not associates Client: Nike Description: Interior graphics at Nike's new store on the Champs Elysees in Paris. The project includes a typographic lift, graphic shoe walls, a display of historic Nike t-shirts, changing room graphics and interior glass walls with graphic images.

Toby Neilan
London, UK

Title: - Designer: Y-3 Client: Y-3
Description: Kabarets Prophecy club in London held the launch for Y-3 A/W'04 collection, where the designer's artwork was installed on the ceiling. The models were photographed so as to appear to be falling from the sky. Scattered on the floor of the club were images of Y-3 accessories printed on vinyl.

HARRIMANSTEEL

London, UK

Title: Footwear Display Designer: Julian Dickinson Client: Nike Description: Point of sale material for Nike to be used in office footwear stores. The design was screen printed onto Perspex formed sheets. Retelling the story of the origin of the product. Taking reference from the bare foot running runners of the rift valley.

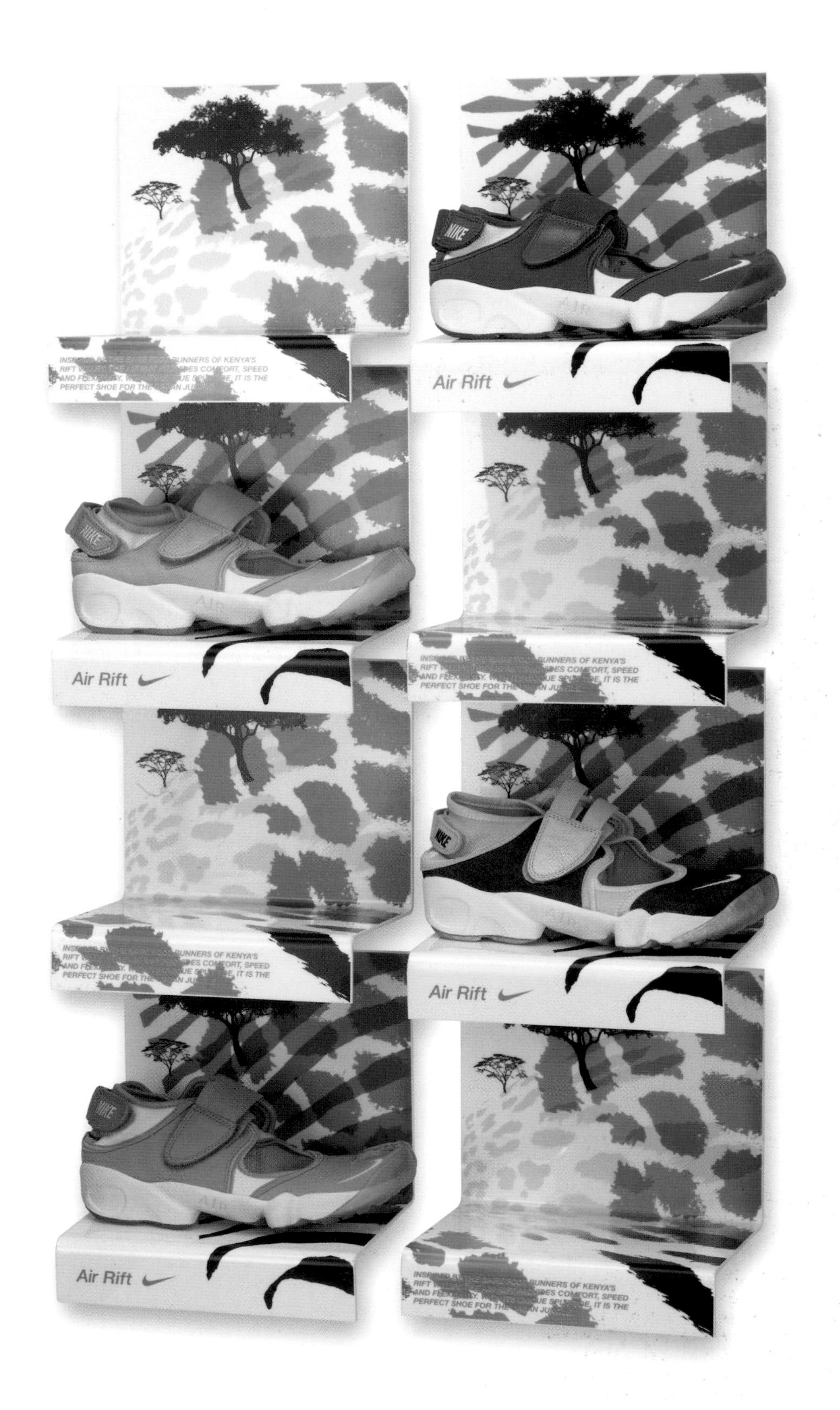
Air Rift
Air Rift
Air Rift
Air Rift

PUMA

Athletics
For
PUMA

PUMA

PUMA

New York, USA

Title: Athletics for Puma Designer: Jason Gnewikow, Matt Owens Client: Puma Description: Puma asked Athletics to develop a series of graphics to be featured on limited edition t-shirts to be sold in Puma stores in the US and Europe. Postcards, stickers and other printed materials were also created. The concept they developed was to provide the client with a few different visual treatments that they felt captured different attitudes of the brand. For example, Athletics used imagery of broken sports equipment as a way of talking about the toughness of sports while also making the designs more interesting by using the forms as overlapping patterns to make unexpected juxtapositions. They also developed 'I heat Puma' imagery to shift the brand message to a more light-hearted concept that was both human and fun. Lastly, they developed a range of pieces using Puma and cat heads to bring out a little humor into the designs.

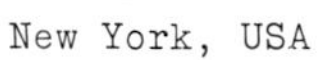

New York, USA

Title: Psyop football scarf Designer: Justin Fines Client: Psyop Description: New York City-based motion graphics juggernaut Psyop contracted Justin Fines to design a classic football scarf which would be given away as a holiday present to their employees and clients. Justin re-interpreted the Psyop 'egg' logo by depicting a cartoonish hand cracking out of the egg holding a paintbrush wet with it's own yolk. Neat!

DEMO

New York, USA

Title: JAM Project t-shirts Designer: Justin Fines Client: JAM of NOW.COM.HK Description: 'Share... feel better' t-shirt project invites the community to share their message via an object in everyday life: t-shirt. Through collaborations with creators from around the world, this project injects the positive messages for everybody in the community; community is then your media. Your style and thoughts, feelings and greetings are transformed into part of your everyday wearable. You can share it simply by wearing it and someone feel better. Demo created two shirts: 'Wasted Youth' and 'Elephant' for the project.

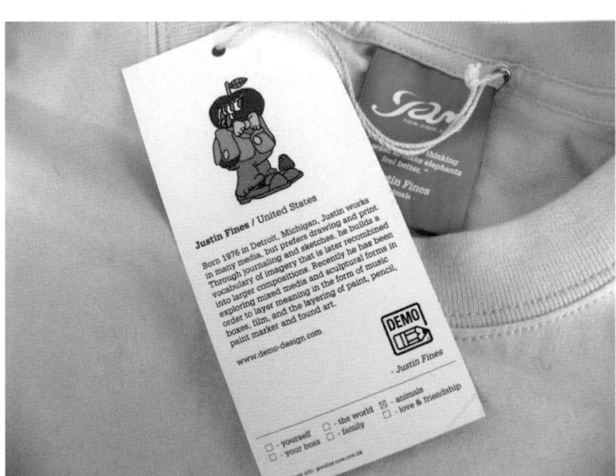

HKI
4GLORY
AIGHT
HKI
4GLORY
TM

*

HKI
4GLORY
TM

**

**

(HKI) HELLOHIKIMORI

Paris, France

* Title: - Designer: David Rondel Cambou Client: GRANIPH Description: T-shirt collection for a Japanese brand, Graniph. (HKI) HELLOHIKIMORI created 4 t-shirts and decided to use it as wallpaper for their office too, sized in 3m x 2m.

** Title: - Designer: David Rondel Cambou Client: WOLFPACK Description: T-shirt collection for an Australian brand, String Republic. (HKI) HELLOHIKIMORI created 2 t-shirts and made special shoot of themselves in use of it in their demo reel.

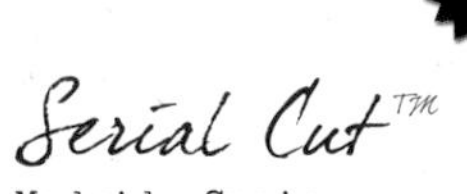

Serial Cut™

Madrid, Spain

Title: Nike Jordan Limited Edition Designer: idem Client: NIKE Jordan USA Description: Graphics for limited edition t-shirts for Nike. Nike USA asked different designers from around the world to create four graphics with a retro feel, telling the story of the NBA's best player ever, Michael Jordan. The aim was to represent Jordan's incredible presence on the court. Serial Cut™ drew retro-basket elements in pencil together with portraits of him from different moments. The prototypes, which are shown on the website, are intended for guys from the ages of 15 to 21. Carry on the Jordan legacy!

23
AIR JORDAN
AIR

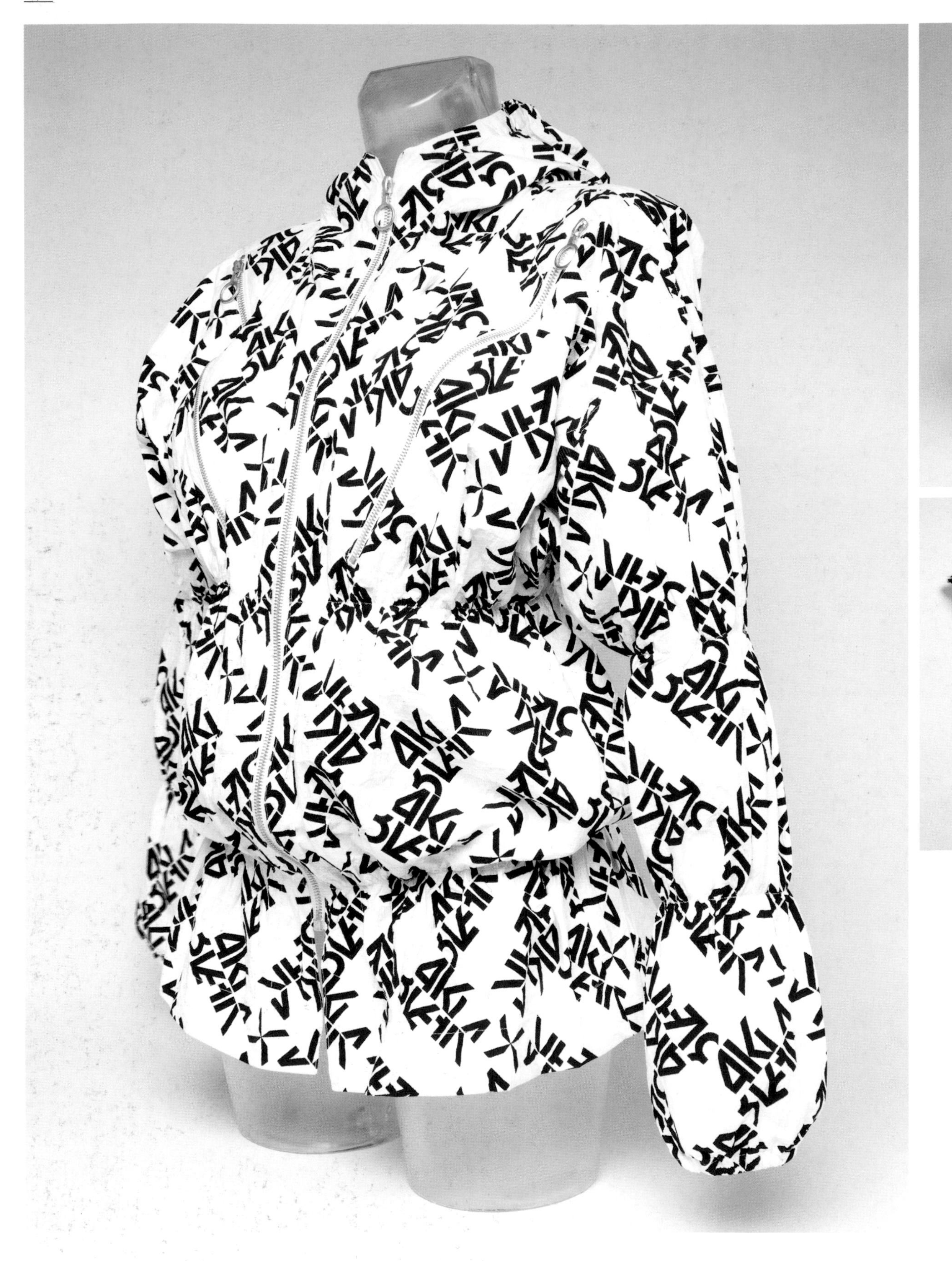

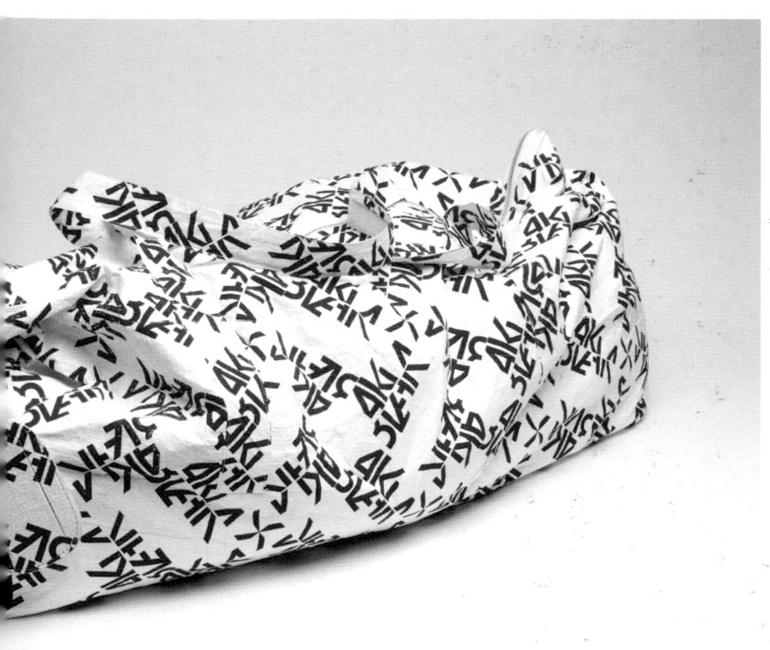

Saturday London

London, UK

<u>Title:</u> Blaak <u>Designer:</u> Saturday <u>Client:</u> Blaak <u>Description:</u> Price tag, clothes tag, textile prints, etc. for Blaak.

Deutschland, Germany

Title: AF 25 Type Treatments Designer: HORT
Client: NIKE, USA Basketball Description: Hort was responsible for the development of a special font and several type treatments to be used on different media.

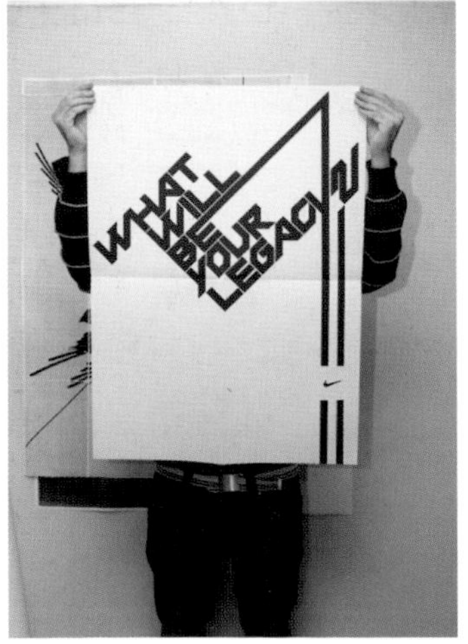

THE
NIKE
LEGACY

FUTURE

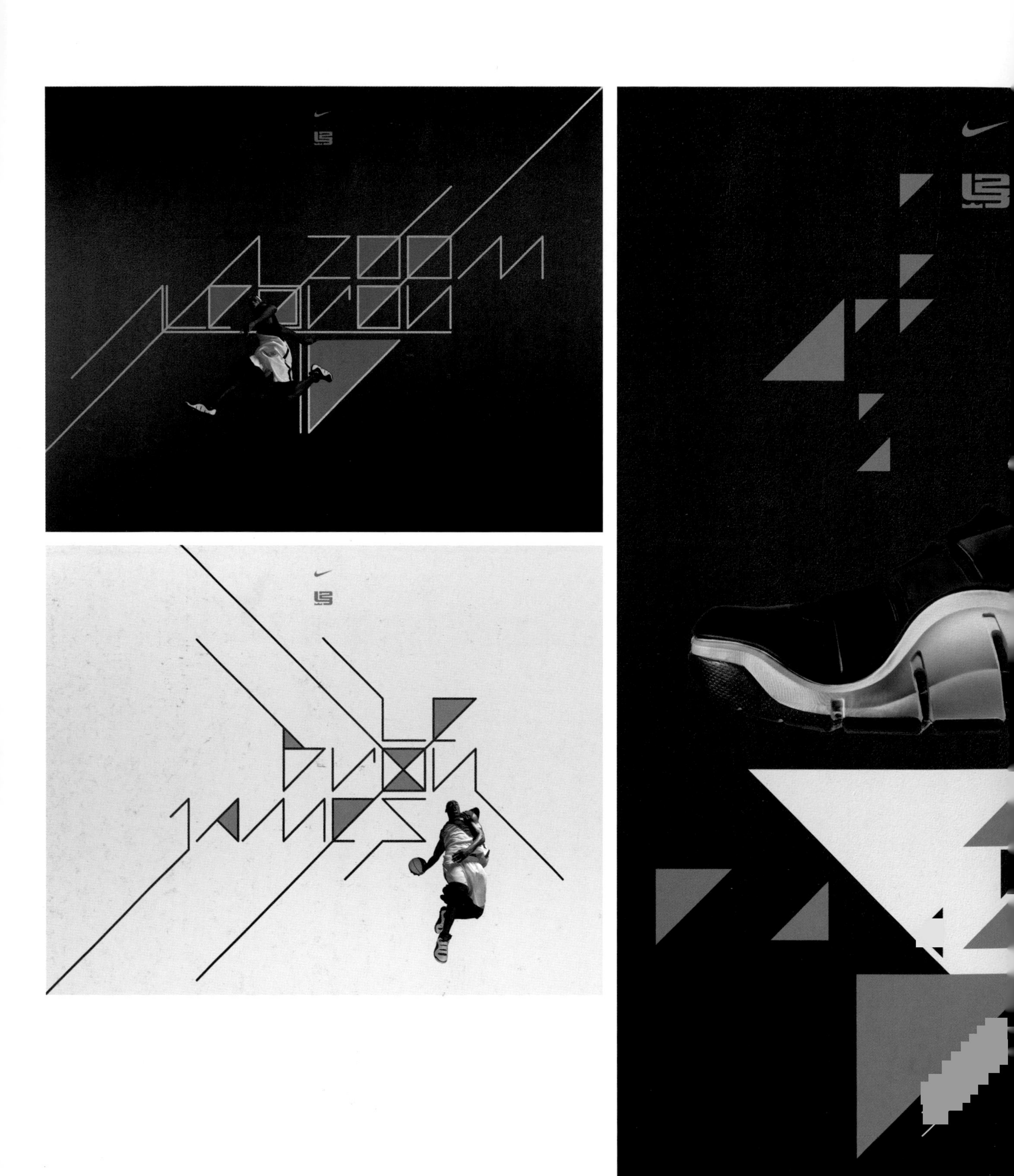

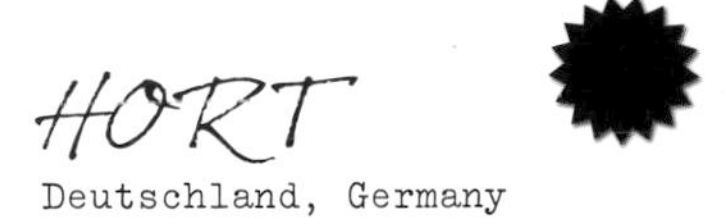

Deutschland, Germany

Title: Le Bron James / Visual Center Designer: HORT Client: NIKE, USA Basketball Description: Hort was responsible for the development of a special font, several type of treatments, graphic language, photo-illustration style, retail programs, fashion, motion graphics, shop window designs, etc. and also the design of the visual center book, design of posters, etc.

LEBRON

LEBRON
LEBRON

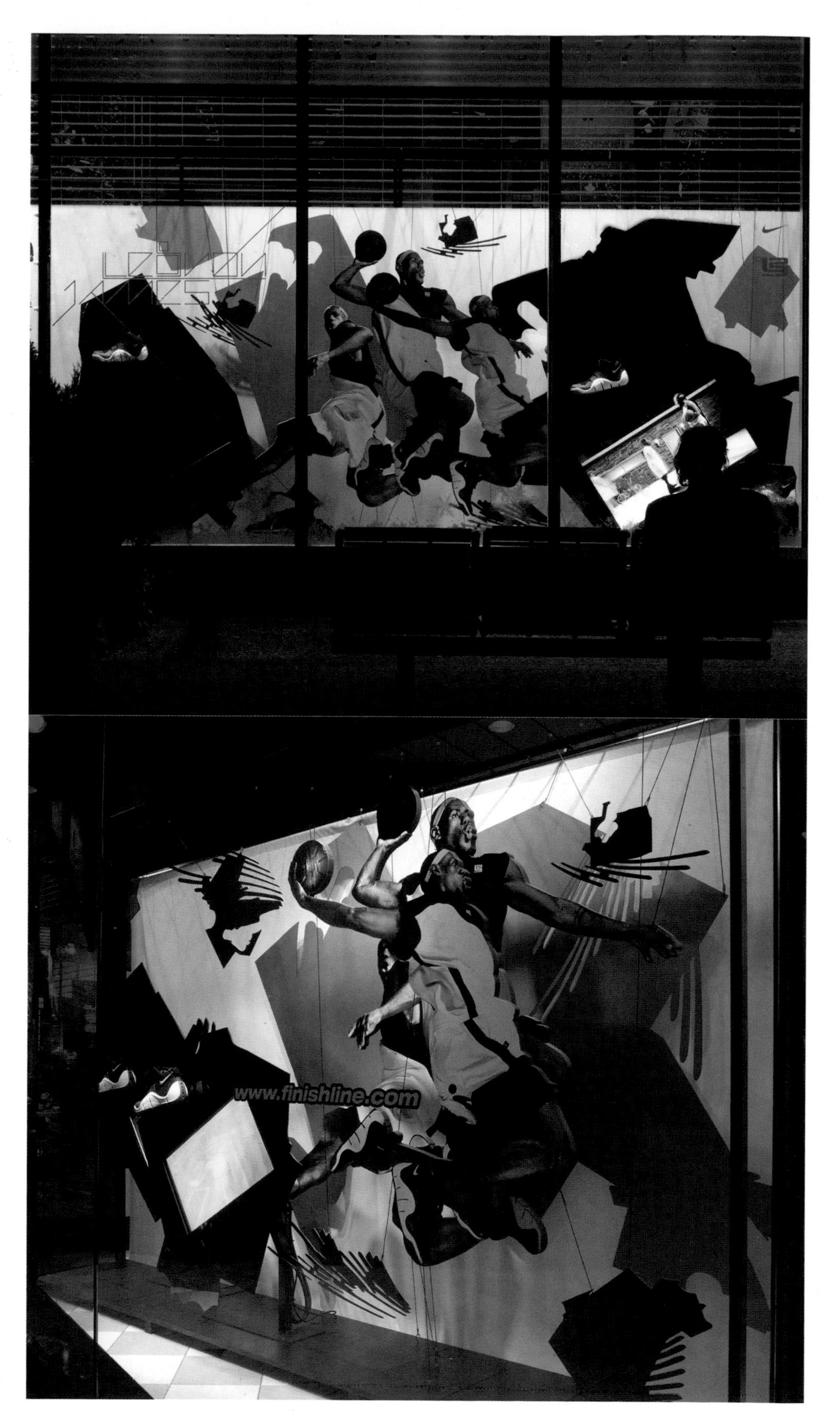

HORT

Deutschland, Germany

Title: Le Bron James / Visual Center Designer: HORT Client: NIKE, USA Basketball Description: Hort was responsible for the development of a special font, several type of treatments, graphic language, photo-illustration style, retail programs, fashion, motion graphics, shop window designs, etc. and also the design of the visual center book, design of posters, etc.

www.finishline.com

OLD PLAYER AS C
MEAN, HIS ALL-A
EXPLOSIVENESS C
GAME, HIS SIGHT
OLD LIKE HIM. HE
PLAYERS BEFORE
GEORGE WASHING
WHO HAVE THE CLE
AND DANGER ALIKE
IT." THUCYDIDES.
INTRODUCTION STATEMENT
LJ VC IV
"IT'S LIKE I SEE THINGS BEFORE THEY H

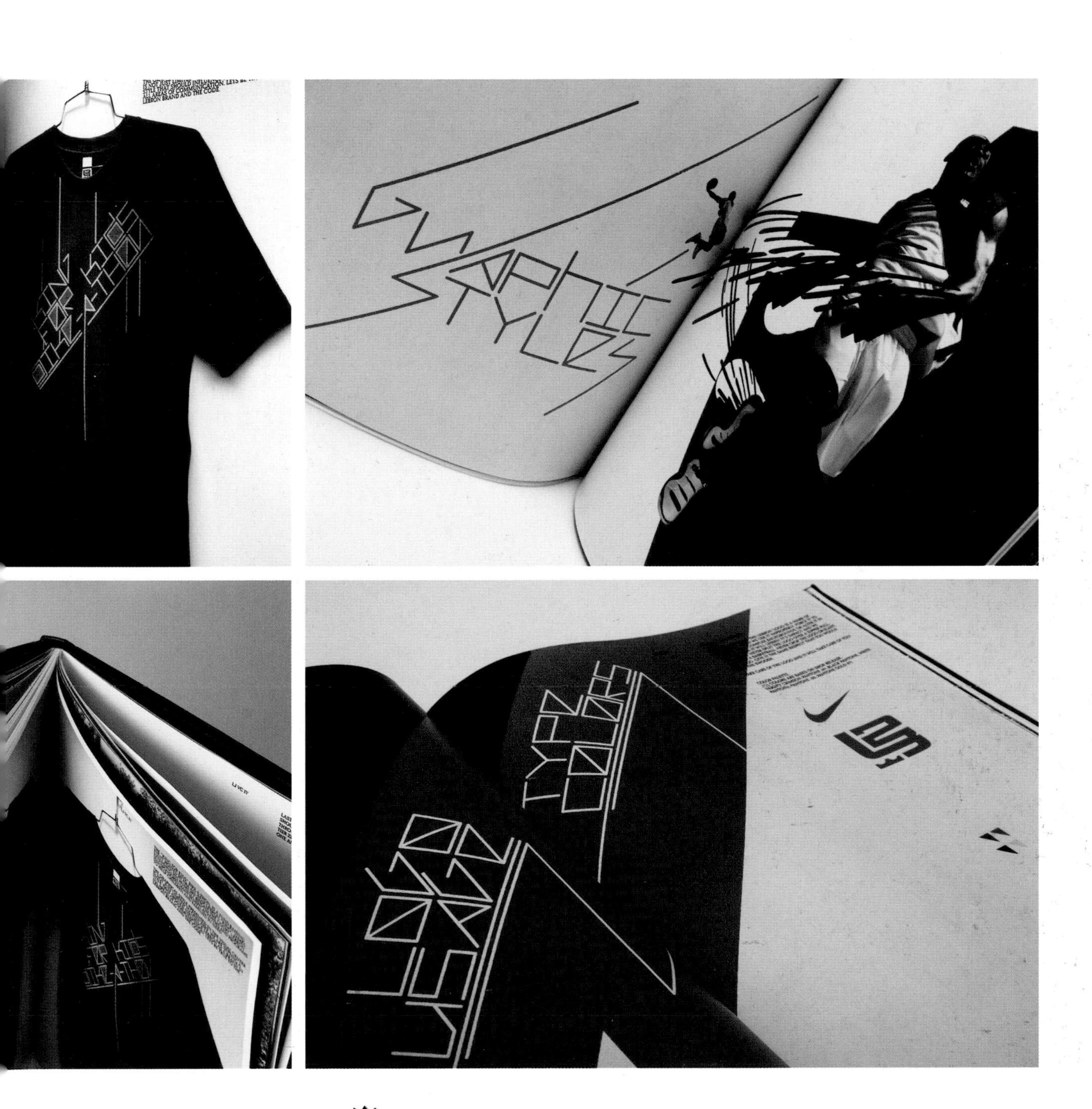

HORT

Deutschland, Germany

Title: Le Bron James / Visual Center Designer: HORT Client: NIKE, USA Basketball Description: Hort was responsible for the development of a special font, several type of treatments, graphic language, photo-illustration style, retail programs, fashion, motion graphics, shop window designs, etc. and also the design of the visual center book, design of posters, etc.

HORT

Deutschland, Germany

Title: Le Bron James / Visual Center Designer: HORT Client: NIKE, USA Basketball Description: Hort was responsible for the development of a special font, several type of treatments, graphic language, photo-illustration style, retail programs, fashion, motion graphics, shop window designs, etc. and also the design of the visual center book, design of posters, etc.

Notausgang
freihalten!

nike.com.sg

BORN FROM OBSESSION
by

BORN FROM
OBSESSION
by

nike.com.sg

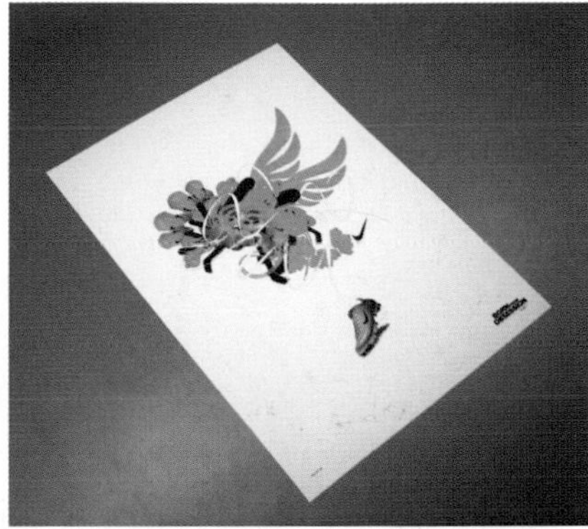

Kinetic Design & Advertising, Singapore

Singapore

Title: Born from Obsession Designer: Jonathan Yuen Client: Nike Inc. Description: Born from Obsession is a recently launched campaign in which Nike introduced a series of high performance sport shoes. The concept of the campaign is 'obsession' and by showing individual parts of the shoes Nike hopes to highlight their commitment to details. Hence, Born from Obsession. Three original campaign posters are designed based on the parts that make up these unique Nike shoes, each representing the key attributes of Freedom, Speed and Precision.

Plazm Media, Inc.

Oregon, Portland

Title: '5678' Designer: Todd Houlette, Eric Mast Client: Nike Description: A campaign focused on dance fitness. Specifically targeted urban women in the Asia Pacific market.

Coverup
This stretch terry, hooded top has an adjustable cord at the back of the hood for extra security. The mesh detailing down the arm matches the woven hip-hop pants.
Hip-Hop Messenger
The Hip-Hop Messenger bag features a magnetic closure to easily access contents, with an exterior zippered pocket to access personal items. Personal items can also be secured within the interior zippered pocket. Shoulder strap is adjustable and can be custom fit. The bag is fully lined to provide a smooth look and feel inside the bag.

Nike Shox Rhythmic
This shoe is for the "gym-diva" who participates in a variety of trendy, new workouts. The durable upper offers protection for dance movements. It is also double lasted for lateral support. A breathable mesh tongue and large open mesh create maximum breathability. It has triangular columns for ultimate stability. The circular columns provide great cushioning and a smooth transition when jumping and stomping. It has a non-stick and non-marking outsole with a pivot point and flex grooves for dance movement. The Duralon pod was included for enhanced cushioning.

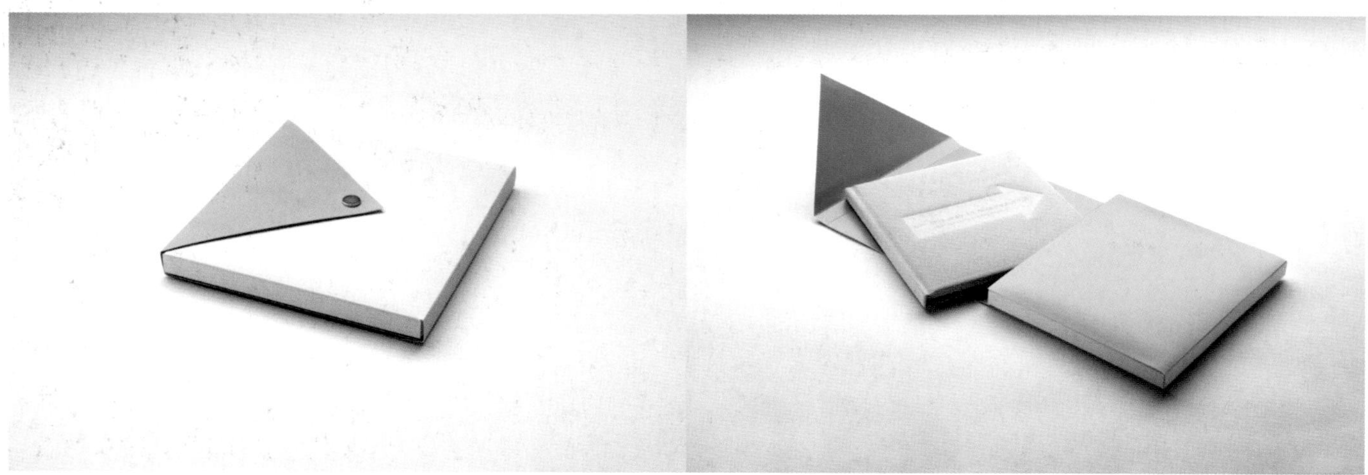

Plazm Media, Inc.

Oregon, Portland

Title: 'This Way to Nike Beautiful' Designer: Todd Houlette, Eric Mast Client: Nike Description: Packaging, publicity and promotional materials for a 2-day media launch of the newest Nike Women's products. Plazm's duties in this project included design of the event space, product displays, directional signage, creation of a 60-page case bound book, design and manufacture of custom-made lavender eye pillows, stickers, magnets, window clings, stationery, PowerPoint templates, CD packaging, among other things.

this way to nikebeautiful

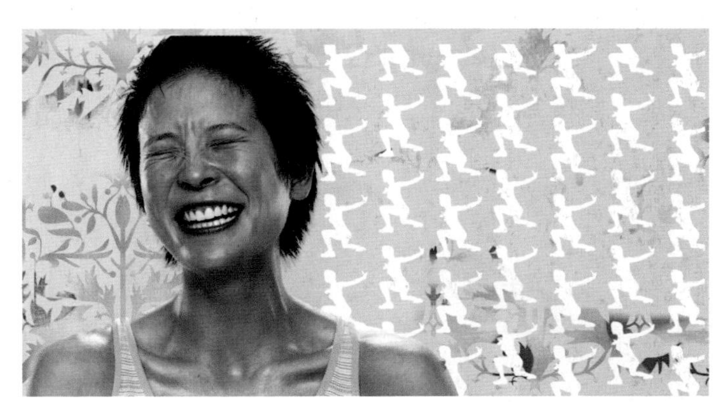

Illdesigners - Power
Inspiration

"Every part of her body and soul awakens as she starts her exercise. She begins by stretching, reaching out with her arms, she jumps, dancing, as she leaps and spreads her rainbow. With her Power, she floats and touches the sky."

MODULAR OUTSOLE
INTERLOCKING MIDSOLE

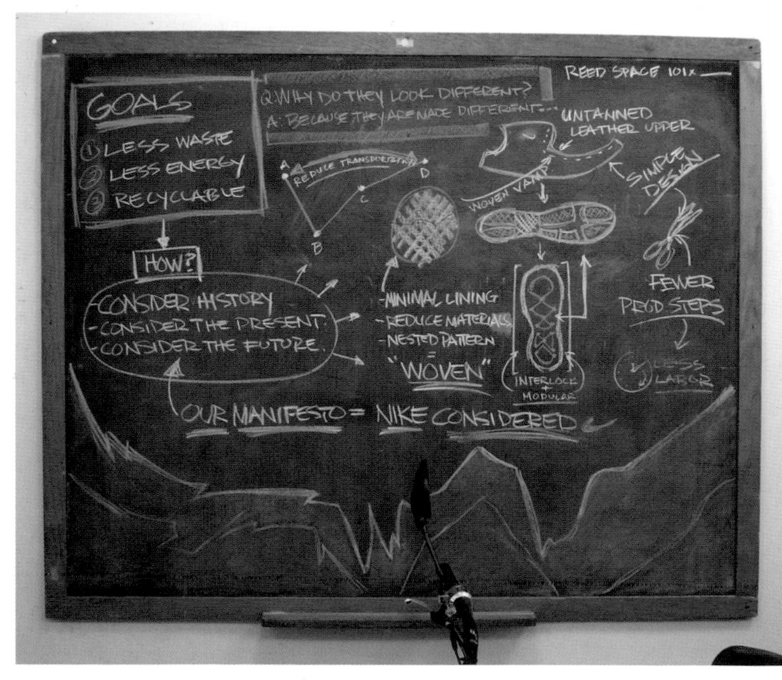
REED SPACE 101x
GOALS
1 LESS WASTE
2 LESS ENERGY
3 RECYCLABLE
Q: WHY DO THEY LOOK DIFFERENT?
A: BECAUSE THEY ARE MADE DIFFERENT...
UNTANNED LEATHER UPPER
REDUCE TRANSPORTATION
A
B
C
D
WOVEN VAMP
SIMPLE DESIGN
HOW?
-CONSIDER HISTORY
-CONSIDER THE PRESENT.
-CONSIDER THE FUTURE.
-MINIMAL LINING
-REDUCE MATERIALS
-NESTED PATTERN
=
"WOVEN"
INTERLOCK + MODULAR
FEWER PROD STEPS
LESS LABOR
OUR MANIFESTO = NIKE CONSIDERED

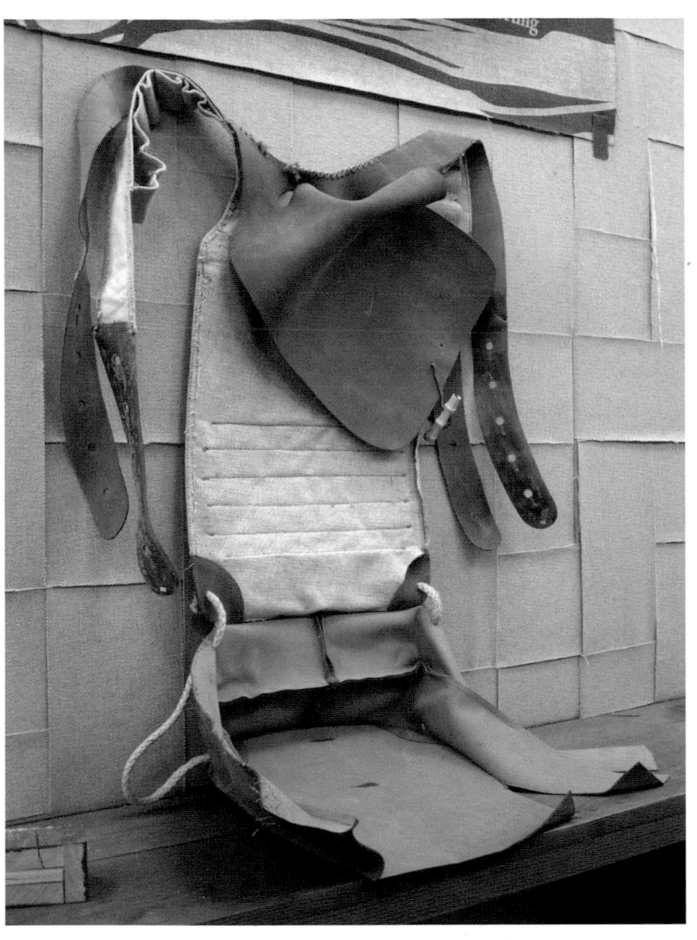

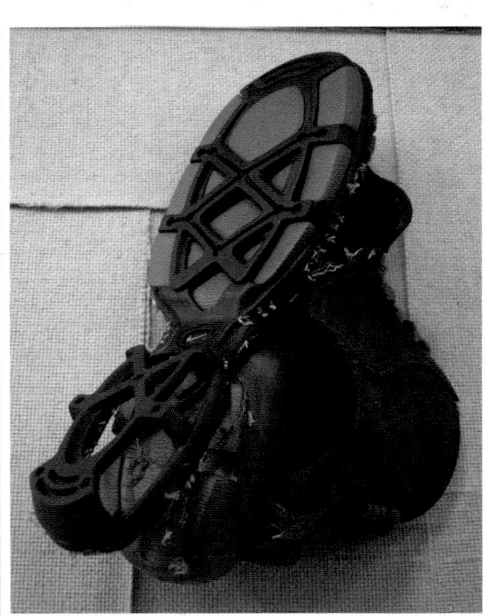

Staple Design

New York, USA

Title: Nike Considered Designer: Staple Design Team Client: Nike Inc. Description: A true A-Z project. Nike came to Staple Design two years prior to the release of this collection to talk about an environmentally sustainable way of making shoes. Staple Design worked with them every step of the way from design to wear testing to retail. Store and Reed Space of Staple Design was the exclusive launch site of the Considered Project.

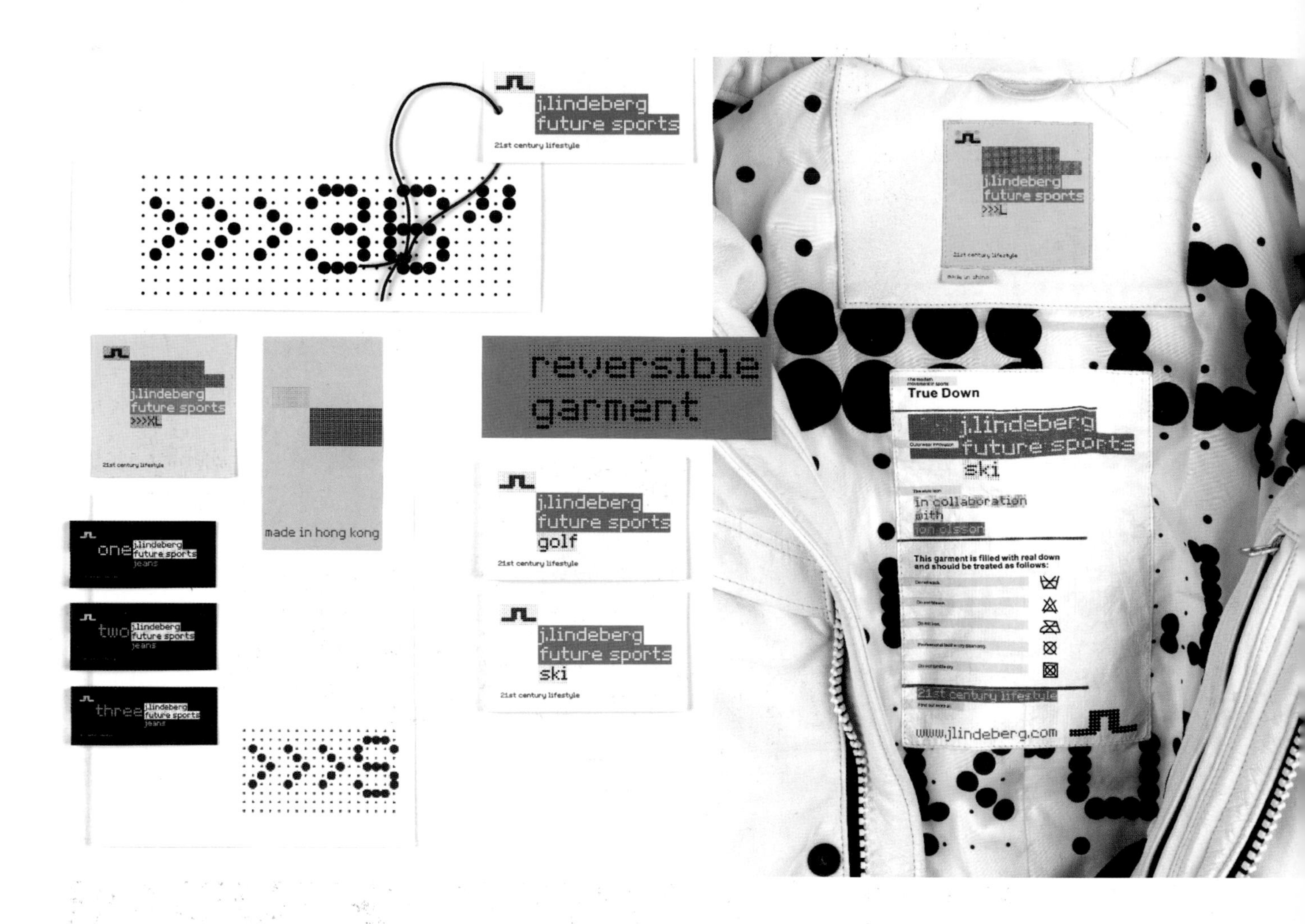
j.lindeberg
future sports
21st century lifestyle
reversible
garment
j.lindeberg
future sports
>>>XL
21st century lifestyle
made in hong kong
one
j.lindeberg
future sports
jeans
two
three
golf
ski
True Down
in collaboration
with
jon olsson
This garment is filled with real down and should be treated as follows:
21st century lifestyle
www.jlindeberg.com

profile
camilo villegas
look as
good as your
game
>

London, UK

Title: J.Linderberg Future Sports Designer: Saturday Client: J.Linderberg Description: Print ads, packaging, etc. promotional materials for J.Linderberg Future Sports.

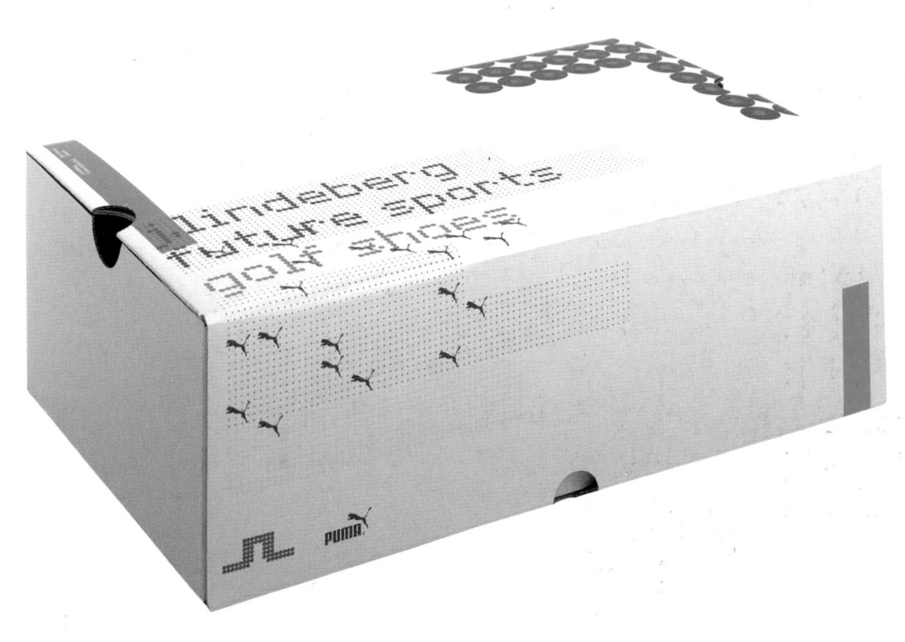

*

**

outasight Co., Ltd.

Tokyo, Japan

* Title: sureshot '05 S/S works 'IRIE' Designer: aka Hal Yamagiwa Client: Journal Standard (Japan), Cannabis (Japan), BLEND Guerrilla Store (Amsterdam) Description: The theme - 'IRIE', is a Jamaican patois word that means 'feeling great.' In it, the designer tried to mix hot street style with Caribbean modern style and this time he designed textile named by Jamaican camouflage.

** Title: sureshot '05-'06 A/W works 'C.R.E.A.M - Cash Rules Everything Around Me.' Designer: aka Hal Yamagiwa Client: Journal Standard (Japan), Cannabis (Japan), BLEND Guerrilla Store (Amsterdam) Description: This collection is inspired by Wu-Tang Clan's classic song 'C.R.E.A.M - Cash Rules Everything Around Me.' The designer expressed C.R.E.A.M to design moneyflage - wearing this coat; you feel you are ruled over the money.

*** Title: sureshot '07 S/S works 'Space is the Place.' Designer: aka Hal Yamagiwa Client: Journal Standard (Japan), Cannabis (Japan), BLEND Guerrilla Store (Amsterdam) Description: Inspired by innovative jazz artist, Sun Ra's cult film, 'Space is the Place,' the designer tried to flavour street fashion with galaxy, space atmosphere. He designed 3D textile named 'Galactic 3D print' and you can see 3D stars using attached red & blue sunglass.

New York, USA

Title: Deanne Cheuk Clothing
Designer: Deanne Cheuk Client: Deanne Cheuk for Three Gee Co.
Description: T-shirt and Sneaker design as part of a full collection of clothing for the Japanese namesake of the brand 'Deanne Cheuk'. The hangtag and woven label are based on Deanne's love of mushrooms and sense of humor.

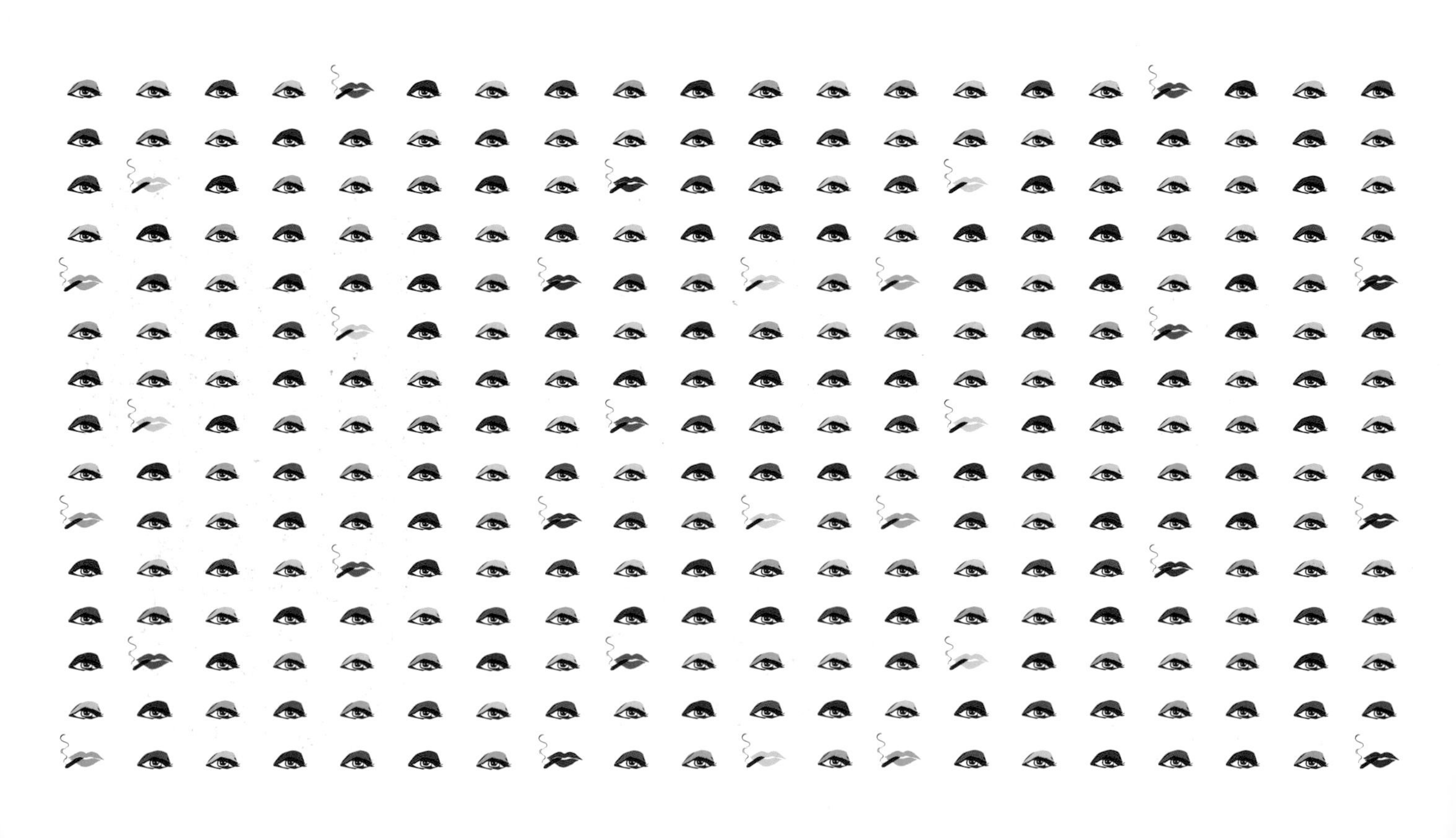

Fedoralime AMFC

New York, USA

Title: G-Unit Clothing Company Campaign Fall 2004 Designer: Brian Mackin Photographer: Anthony Mandler Client: G-Unit Clothing Company / Marc Ecko Enterprises Description: A seasonal fashion campaign 'The 50th Brigade' - This campaign was developed around the tagline 'Becoming A Man Is The Reward.' In this campaign the older G-Unit members put young boys through a 'Survival Of The Fittest' boot camp.

The 50th Brigade
DETERMINATION BUILDS CHARACTER
BECOMING A MAN IS THE REWARD
G Unit
CLOTHING COMPANY
G-UNIT

The 50th Brigade
TRAINING ACADEMY
DISCIPLINE BEGINS WITH FOCUS
BECOMING A MAN IS THE REWARD
G Unit
CLOTHING COMPANY
g-unitclothing.com

Ipsum Planet

Madrid, Spain

Title: Lois (Spring/Summer 07 Ad Campaign) Designer: Ipsum Planet Photographer: Jm Ferrater Client: Lois Description: Lois is a Spanish jeans brand born in 1962. They sell jeans but also the idea of being Spanish and his experience in fashion during more than 40 years. For those reasons Ipsum Planet have created a campaign with the claim 'Love is Lois;' images with a mix of hippy culture (the sixties, when Lois is born) and religious kitsch (very typical images of Spanish popular culture: Religious engraving). Sixties and religion with a touch of humour and fashion.

Ipsum Planet 06 / Foto: Ferrater
PROUD TO BE
Bull
MADE IN SPAIN
Since
1962
www.loisjeans.com
Lois®

Made

Oslo, Norway

Title: Levi's Designer: Made Client: Levi's and N&D Description: Made was asked to create a set of boards/posters to promote the launch of an art project based on the Levi's AntiFit campaign. Made found all the original campaign material they received unappealing to work with, so they created some their own material. Made came up with the idea of anti-fitting the poster literally, and created artwork based on this.

Crème, a playful colour, is simply delightful. It makes the best canvas for experimental, conceptual and interactive designs. This section shows how its subtle nature allows humour and passion of the image to shine through.

CRÈME

Hong Kong, China

Title: - Designer: Nam Kong Client: this is Description: No complicated concept, no splendid decorations, simple and natural design is always the style of 'this is.' Easy to carry, cuttings and materials are the most essential issues for its designs. Not being waved by the trend yet fashionable, the timeless designs belong to everyone and help bringing out everyone's beauty and unique character.

Hong Kong, China

Title: - Designer: Nam Kong Client: this is Description: No complicated concept, no splendid decorations, simple and natural design is always the style of 'this is'. Easy to carry, cuttings and materials are the most essential issues for its designs. Not being waved by the trend yet fashionable, the timeless designs belong to everyone and help bringing out everyone's beauty and unique character. To present the brand idea of 'Base on man', the designer personally found 6 non-professional yet with exclusive style models for showcasing his designs.

this
is
: tina leung

ZZZ...

Tokyo, Japan

Title: Canon Designer: Kunihiko Morinaga Client: - Description: The concept was to show the shapes of all the letters of the alphabet in the form of clothes and accessories. A cut and sewn took the form of an 'A' when laid flat, while a blouse had its armholes in slightly different places on left and right sides in order to form an 'N.' There was nothing here that seemed too forced, just good-looking everyday clothes distinguished by draping and layering of fabric.

zzz...

Sara Lamúrias Unipessoal Lda (aforest-design)

Amadora, Portugal

Title: odori tabi socks Designer: Sara Lamúrias Client: aforest-design Description: aforest-design presents a limited edition of 100. It is special pairs of odori tabi socks. To wear and to watch, it is available in 5 different viewable natures. There are different themes includes silent snow, autumn leaves, cherry blossoms, volcano and green forest. The tabi are popular among traditional Japanese dancers and theatre artists; you can use them as home shoes or with your sandals.

aforest-design®
printed photo collage on 100% cotton
cherry blossom
odori tabi socks

aforest-design®
printed photo collage on 100% cotton
green forest
odori tabi socks

aforest-design®
printed photo collage on 100% cotton
silent snow
odori tabi socks

aforest-design®
printed photo collage on 100% cotton
volcano
odori tabi socks

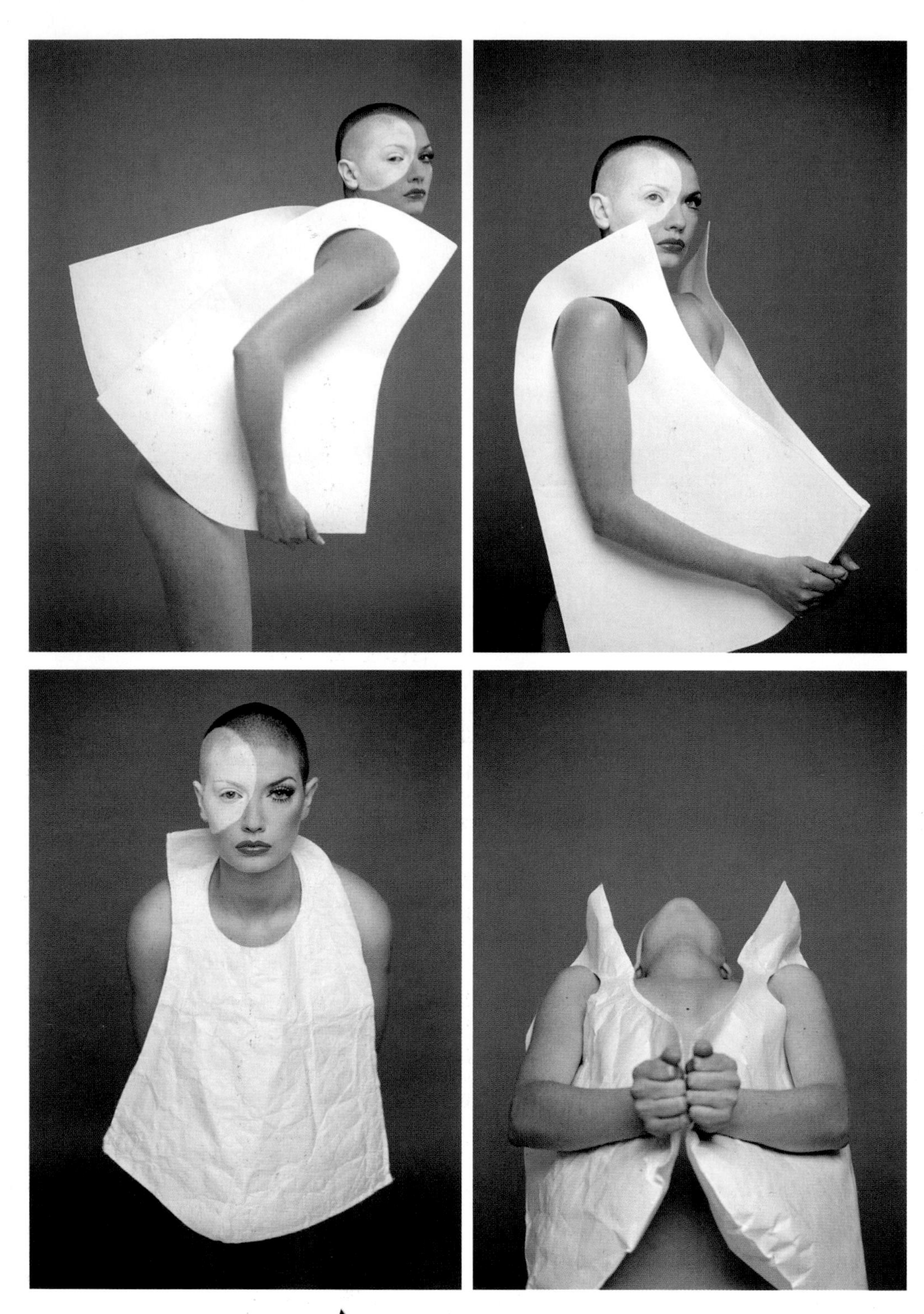

KrvKurva Design

Lisboa, Portugal

Title: La.ga bag Designer: Daniela Pais, Jorge Moita Photographer: Ricardo Cruz at Lemon Space Client: - Description: La.Ga is a bag made to be dressed. She transforms itself into a part of you and changes your silhouette like a new perspective integrated into your body. In opposition to fashion accessories and to the way these are apart from the body. She is dynamic, processing gradual changes in its shape and texture through time, enduring your lifestyle and becoming something unknown. For all reasons, it raises the question: 'Can we wear anything that surrounds us?,' to which the answer is an absolute yes! More than the fabrics of clothing, it is buildings, cars and furniture pieces that dress us all the time.

KrvKurva Design

Lisboa, Portugal

Title: La.ga bag - To Love Is Not An Option Designer: Daniela Pais, Jorge Moita Photographer: Tatiana Macedo Client: - Description: It is a series of limited editions of 300 pieces, signed by a selection of designers and illustrators, both of international status and local recognition, that interpreted the theme proposed: To Love is Not An Option.

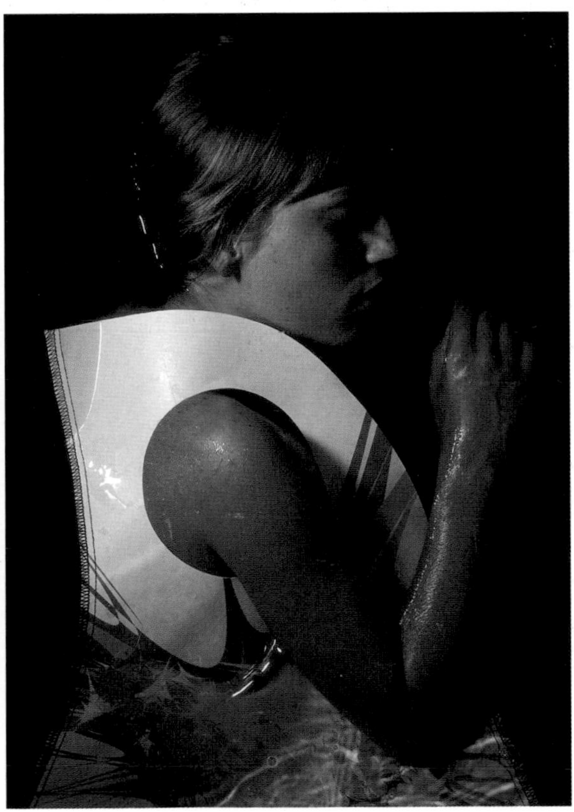

*

**

***

Studio Job
Belgium / The Netherlands

* Title: Charm Chain for Runway Rocks Designer: Studio Job Client: Swarovski Description: Laser cut, drummed aluminum chains and Charm inlayed with Swarovski crystals.

** Title: Charm Chain Designer: Studio Job Client: Viktor & Rolf Description: Laser cut and drummed aluminum chains and Charms.

*** Title: Black Widow Designer: Studio Job Client: Chi Ha Paura Description: Laser cut, drummed and anodized aluminum chains and Charm.

Surface to air. Paris

Paris, France

Title: - Designer: Santiago Marotto, Jeremie Rozan Client: dover street market Description: Dover street market gives young creators a special retail corner on their basement to showcase at the same time special products and creative work. Surface to air has been asked to develop a limited edition t-shirts along with an installation on the assigned retail space. They have brought to London 150 paper made deers that are naturally creating a path to hiding treasure. The idea is to create with a simple element a repetition, a clone that creates a texture a visual effect.

JEDER
FÜR SICH
UND GOTT
GEGEN
ALLE

SURFACE
TO AIR

DRAW
THE SHORT
STRAW

HANDS

Sara Lamúrias Unipessoal Lda (aforest-design)

Amadora, Portugal

Title: tv off the knitted sessions Designer: Sara Lamúrias Client: aforest-design Description: turn off is a statement against dead-end couch and zapping culture. It is about cleaning up the mental environment from distorted news, manipulative advertising, and top-down culture. The goal is simple: to shake up routines and get people questioning the role of TV in their lives. aforest-design is now supporting this movement, with the edition of a knitted pieces collection, evidencing the moments of pause and rest of the TV, practically inexistent nowadays: signal tests, emission interruptions - one hears the national hymn and end... tv off, turn off is pressed. Color scales, shades of light RGB mix are shown in sweaters and jumpers. From head to supermarket bag everything is knitted.

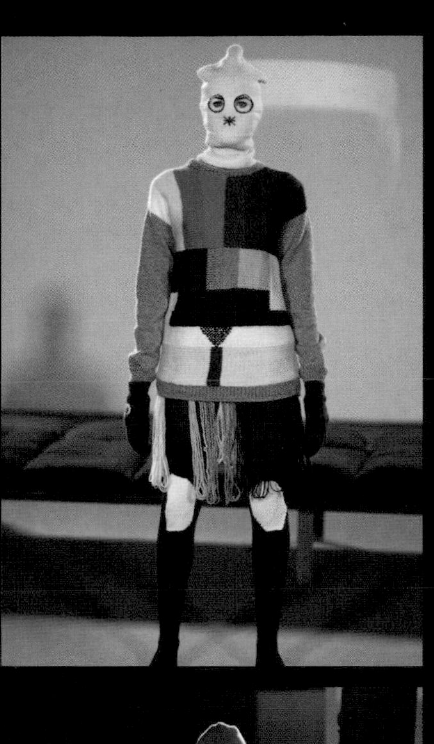

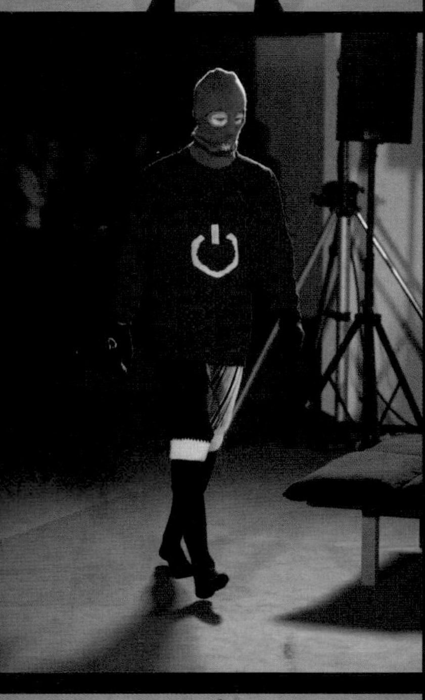
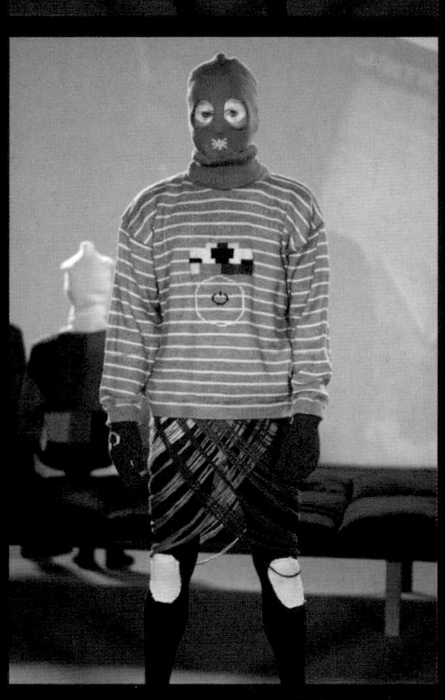

OFF

Edwina Hörl Japan

Tokyo, Japan

Title: KIMONO NO SODE (the kimono's sleeve)
Designer: Edwina Hörl Client: - Description: S/S 06 is a remake collection, possibly in the context of cultural transfer. The title of the collection comes from an essay by the Japanese writer Osamu Dazai explaining the shape of the kimono's sleeve.

One part are of the collection are remake t-shirts, modified in 3 categories: 'sode' sleeve, 'obi' kimono's belt, 'eri' collar.

SODE: Change the t-shirt sleeves to kimono-like sleeves. / OBI: Attaching extra material around the middle to imitate an 'obi.' / ERI: Attaching a material to the front to imitate a kimono's-collar.

The other parts of the collection are antique kimonos, 'tobi' pants (typical Japanese working pants) and 'sukajams' (a short word for 'yokosuka jumpers,' Japanese embroidered blouson jackets). Some of the kimonos are disassembled and modified into a different item like a shirt or skirt. Some of them are presented as they are, but with just the collection's tag attached.

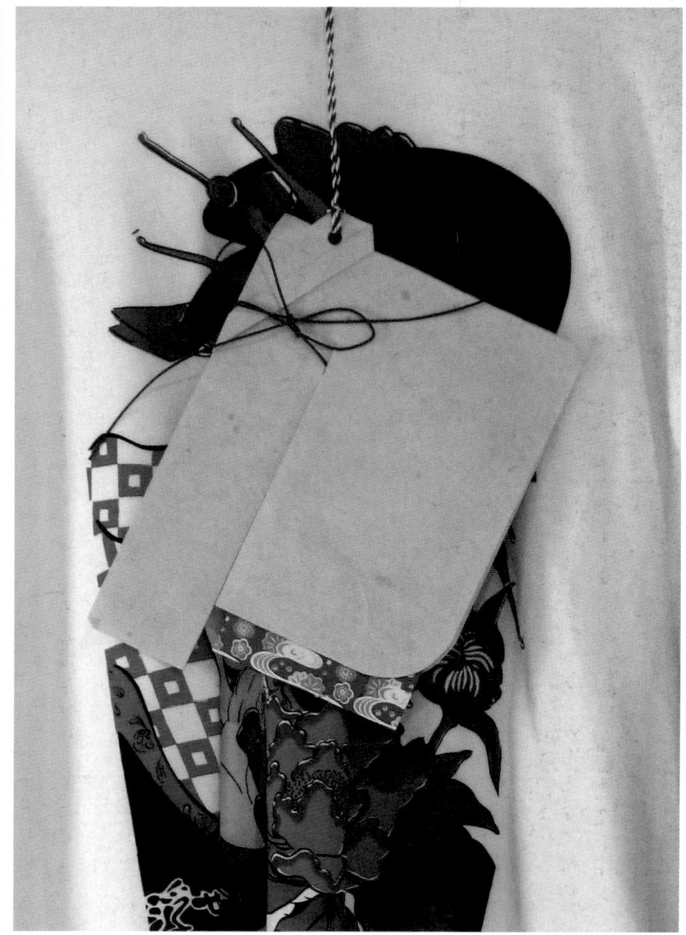

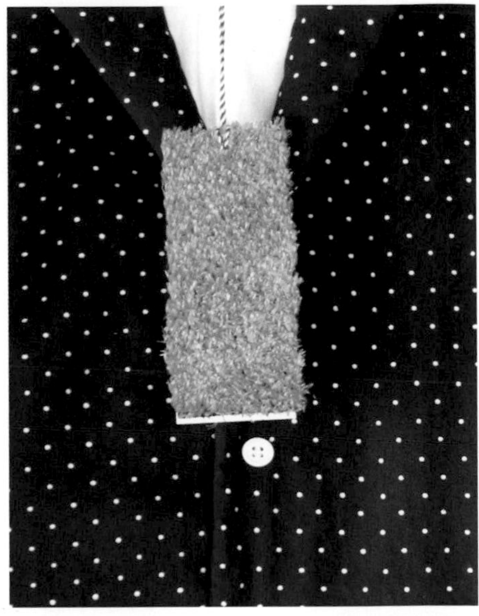

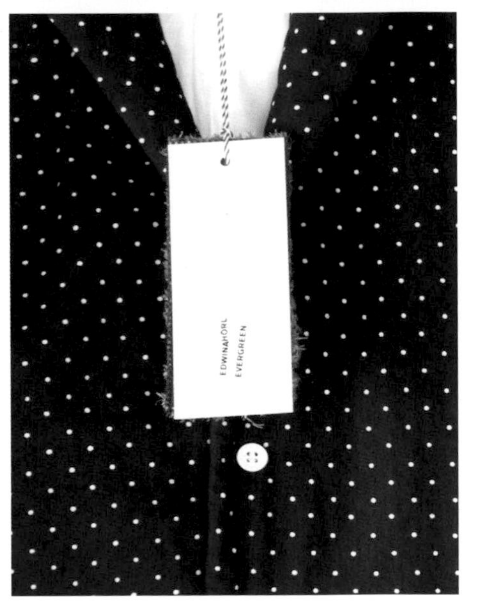

Edwina Hörl Japan

Tokyo, Japan

Title: EVERGREEN Designer: Edwina Hörl Photographer: Seiji Shibuya Client: - Description: AW 06/07 is an 'evergreen' collection, celebrating the start of the brand 'edwina hörl' 10 years ago. It celebrates the rediscovery of Hörl's Austrian culture and multicultural traditions. It embodies a humorous mix of elements from central and eastern European artistic handicraft, like handmade straw shoes from Austria and embroidered fabrics from Czech and Switzerland and traditional indigo dyed blue print fabric from Hungary. The designer picked up clothing themes and silhouettes, that are frequently inspired by what ordinary people wear in these regions, like aprons, the Sunday suit etc. The collection is a review and a preview, containing stories oscillating between 'The Sound of Music' and 'the smile of Japan.'

The text/poem 'tokioblond' by Martin Kubaczek to the booklet goes along with the photos on artificial grass of Seiji Shibuya. Art direction: so+ba

London, UK

* Title: skirt 231 Designer: Alison Willoughby Client: -

** Title: skirt 204 Designer: Alison Willoughby Client: -

Description: Kilt is created out of a length of wool, and that reminds the designer of her use of fabric as a canvas with patterns developed from simple flat shapes. Much of the inspiration for her pieces comes from the places that are neglected, ever-changing, disintegrating and subsiding. She records images through photography, amasses hundreds of stills to dissect then translates into fabric samples, and later into skirts. Once the process is completed, the finished skirts are designed and made by the designer herself. She works in a variety of materials and collects unusual textiles for her work.

*

**

Belgium

Title: 'not for sale' Designer: Koen Geurts, Marenthe Otten, Erik Verdonck Client: erik verdonck Description: The images are collages of the collection 'not for sale' erikverdonck 2006 in collaboration with graphic designers studio 'tbrandtweer.' The images are printed on 100% cotton cousins 80 X 160 cm and presented in cars. The collection was not for sale but people can sit on it. The collages are technical used for the first time in the collections erik verdonck and represent the ego of a/the designer versus his claim to express individuality.

www.erikverdonck.com

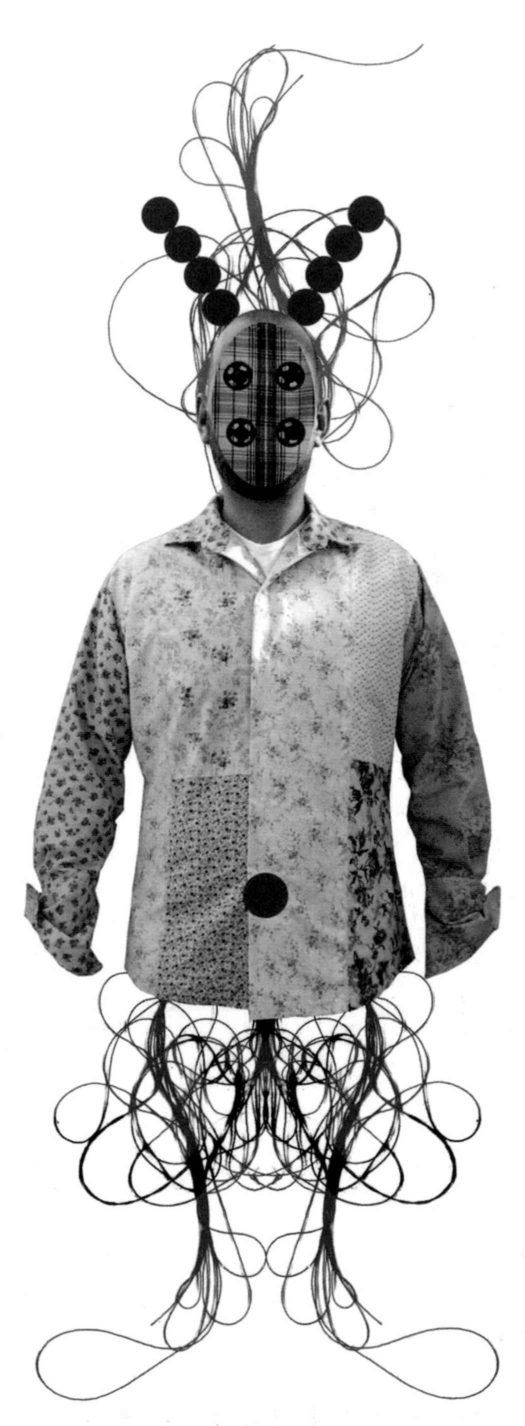
www.erikverdonck.com

Filip Pagowski
New York, USA

* Title: - Designer: - Client: Comme des Garçons Description: Filip Pagowski has a long and spontaneous relationship with Comme des Garcon. Assignments from CdG are always open-ended and have no direction, leaving a lot of freedom for the artist to create. Filip first started working with CdG in late November 1999. The eyes are used for the CdG SHIRT advertisements and more had been selected for season greetings.

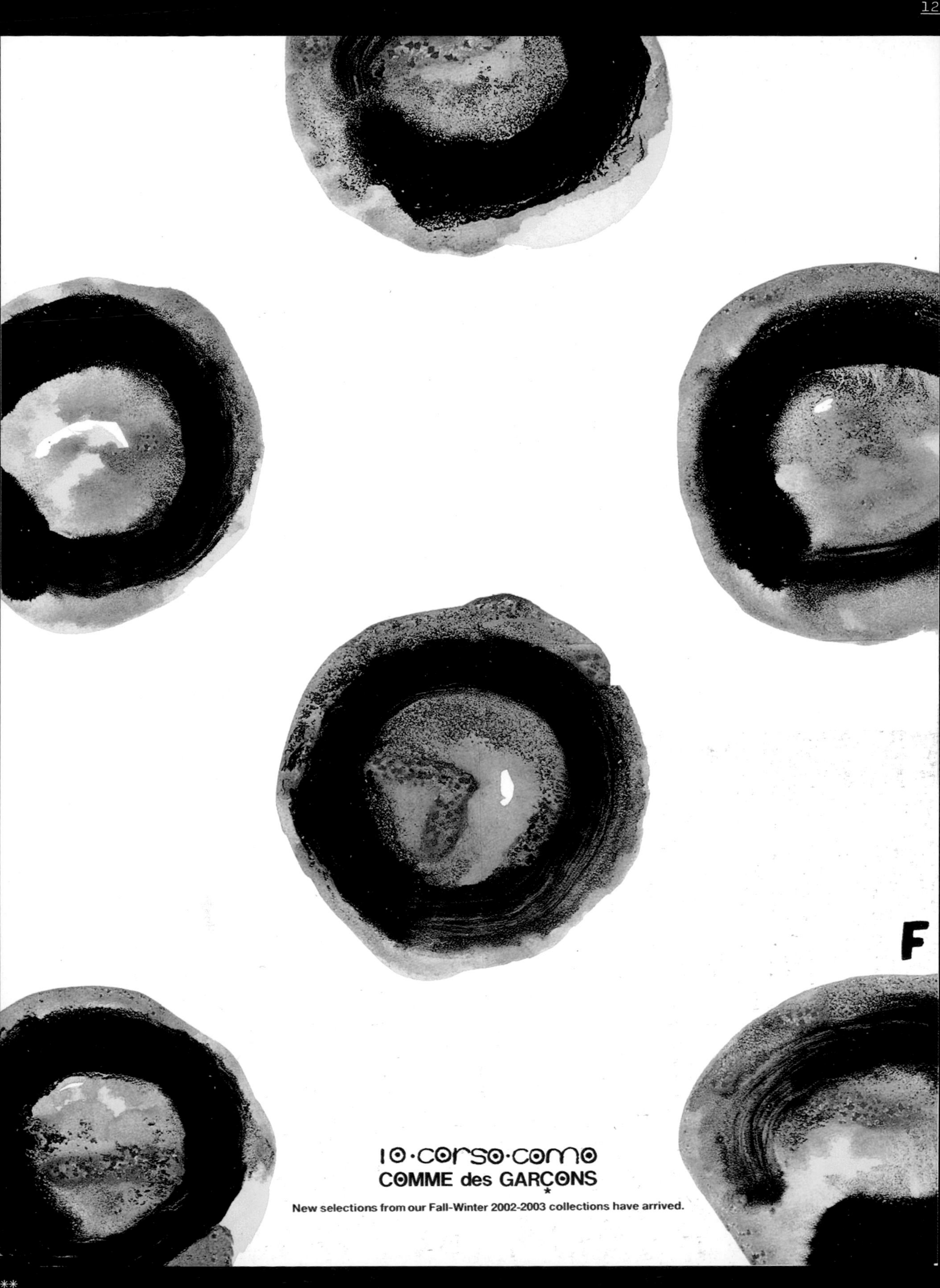
12
F
10·corso·como
COMME des GARÇONS
New selections from our Fall-Winter 2002-2003 collections have arrived.
**

Filip Pagowski
New York, USA

Title: - Designer: - Client: Comme des Garçons Description: The designer was asked to design prints for women's and men's fall 2000 collections, which were inspired by punk movement, but had to be 'updated' with a 2000 look.

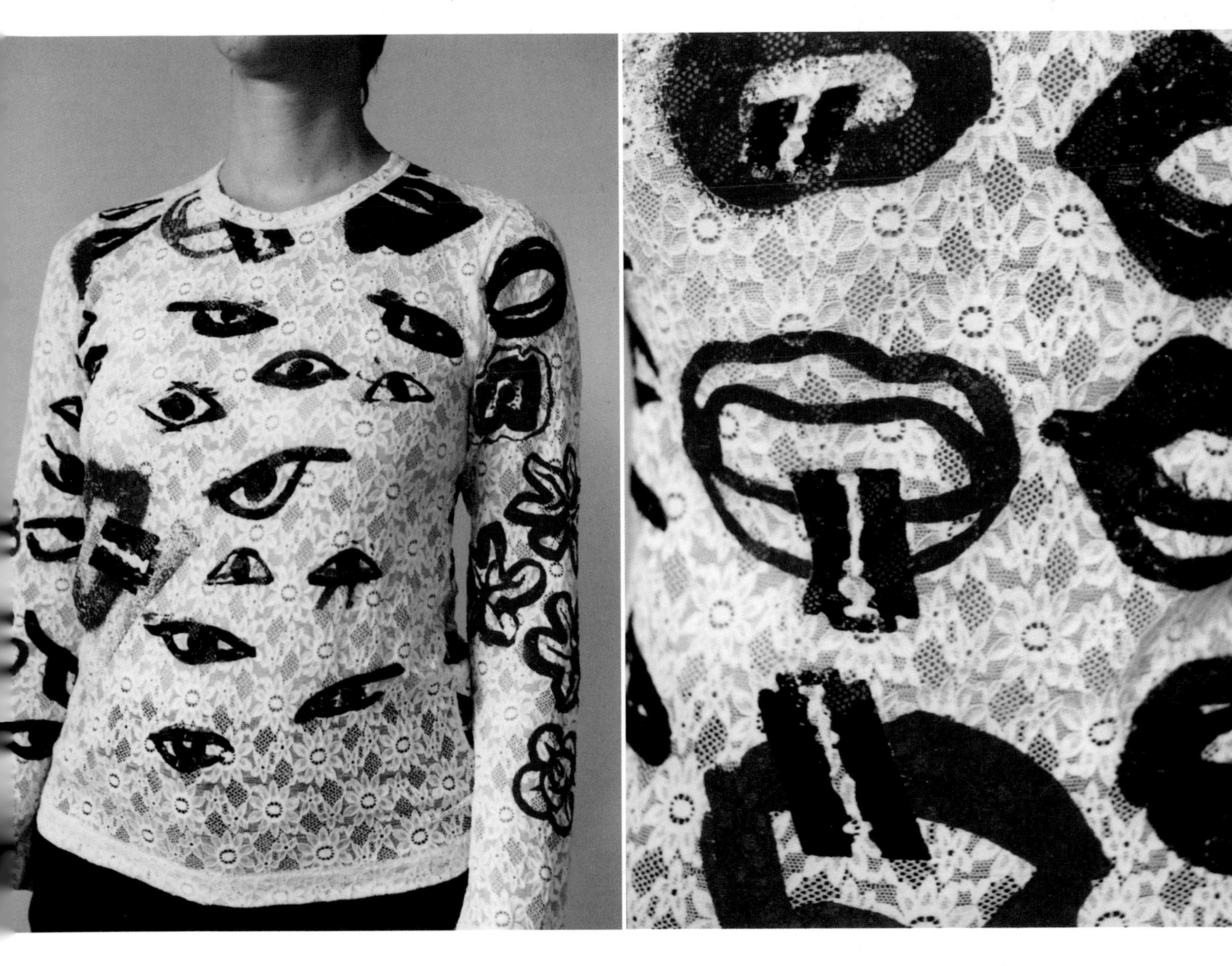

Filip Pagowski

New York, USA

Title: - Designer: - Client: Comme des Garçons Description: The designer was asked to design prints for women's and men's fall 2000 collections, which were inspired by punk movement, but had to be 'updated' with a 2000 look.

Filip Pagowski

New York, USA

Title: - Designer: - Client: Comme des Garçons Description: The designer was asked to design prints for women's and men's fall 2000 collections, which were inspired by punk movement, but had to be 'updated' with a 2000 look.

Filip Pagowski
New York, USA

Title: - Designer: - Client: Comme des Garçons Description: PLAY was conceived in 2002. There were other things like series of scarves for Robe de Chambre line in Japan, numerous greeting cards and announcements for CdG and Corso Como store in Milan and Collette in Paris. One of the last things the designer did was a 'cousin' to the original red PLAY heart logo - the new green one. Recently he worked on visuals for the launch of PLAY perfume.

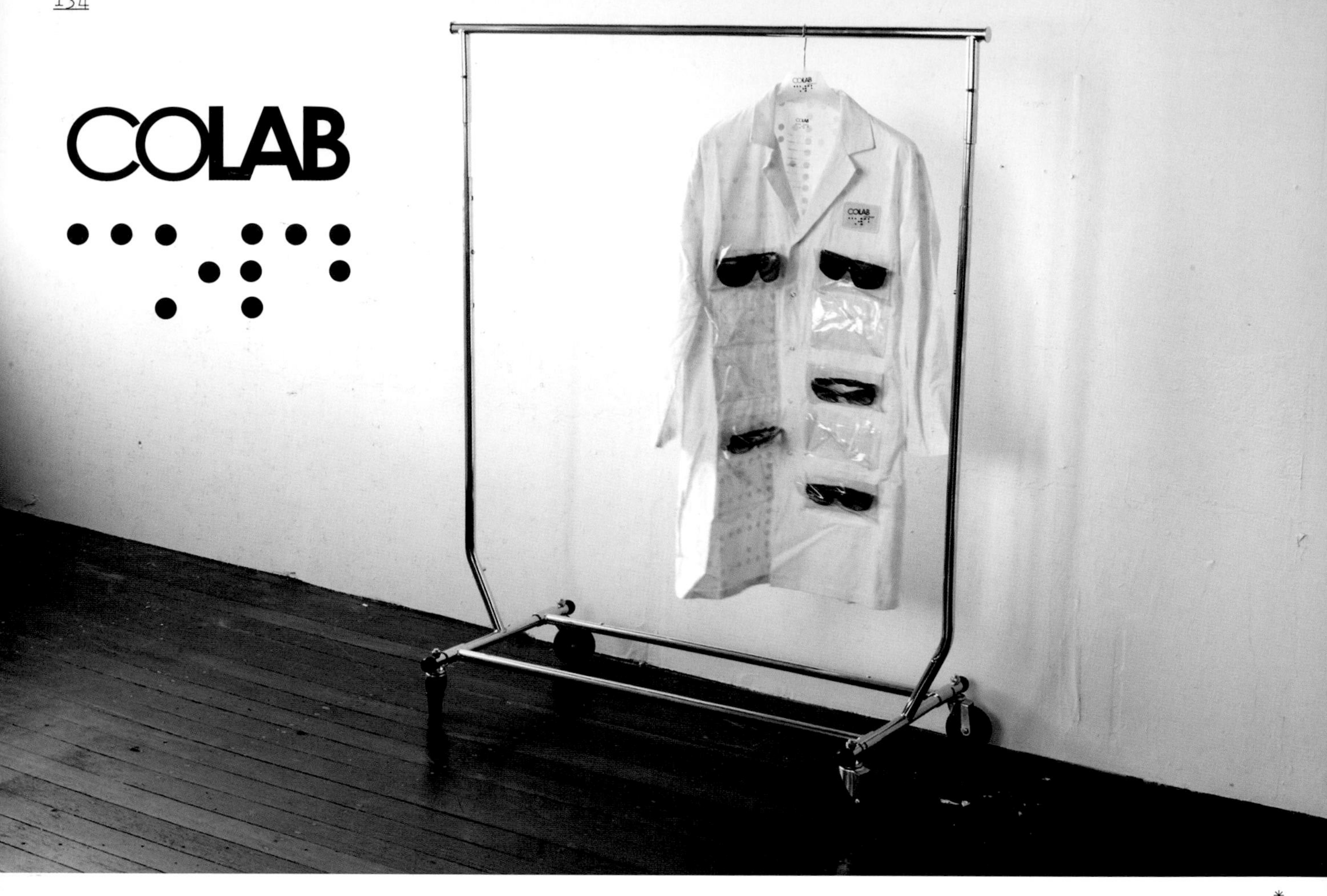

*

Sydney, Australia

* Title: COLAB Logo and COLAB Lab Coat Designer: Dave Allison Client: - Description: The COLAB eyewear logo is designed with a 'tongue in cheek' approach. It merely spells out COLAB in braille. There have been many versions of this logo. Playing upon the theme of 'mad scientist,' the lab coat, originally conceived as a POS device. This is ideal for boutiques and various stores to hang as a feature in store. Its adaptability allows it to hang from a rear wall, store window or central store rack. There is enough space on the front of the jacket in the clear pockets to hang ten COLAB styles with ease. Internally there are 'scientist ID' details printed, for the art-scientist to fill in. COLAB developed a woven label on the front and had specially designed a custom hanger.

** Title: Geoff Mcfetridge x COLAB Designer: Geoff Mcfetridge Client: - Description: COLAB eyewear teamed up with Geoff Mcfetridge to produce a range of limited edition eyewear and related promotional materials.

**

COLAB eyewear

Sydney, Australia

* Title: PAM x COLAB Designer: PAM (PERKS AND MINI), Misha Hollenbach, Shauna Toohey Client: -

** Title: Geoff Mcfetridge x COLAB Designer: Geoff Mcfetridge Client: -

Description: COLAB eyewear teamed up with PAM (PERKS AND MINI) and Geoff Mcfetridge to produce a range of limited edition eyewear. These frames are deemed instant collectibles and available worldwide in the most selective boutique stores.

**

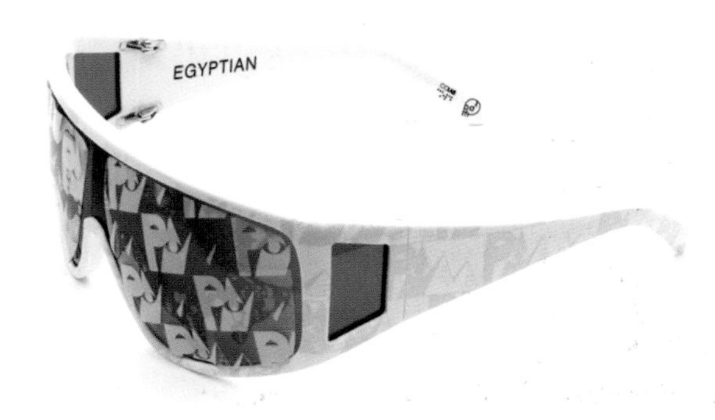

* *

*

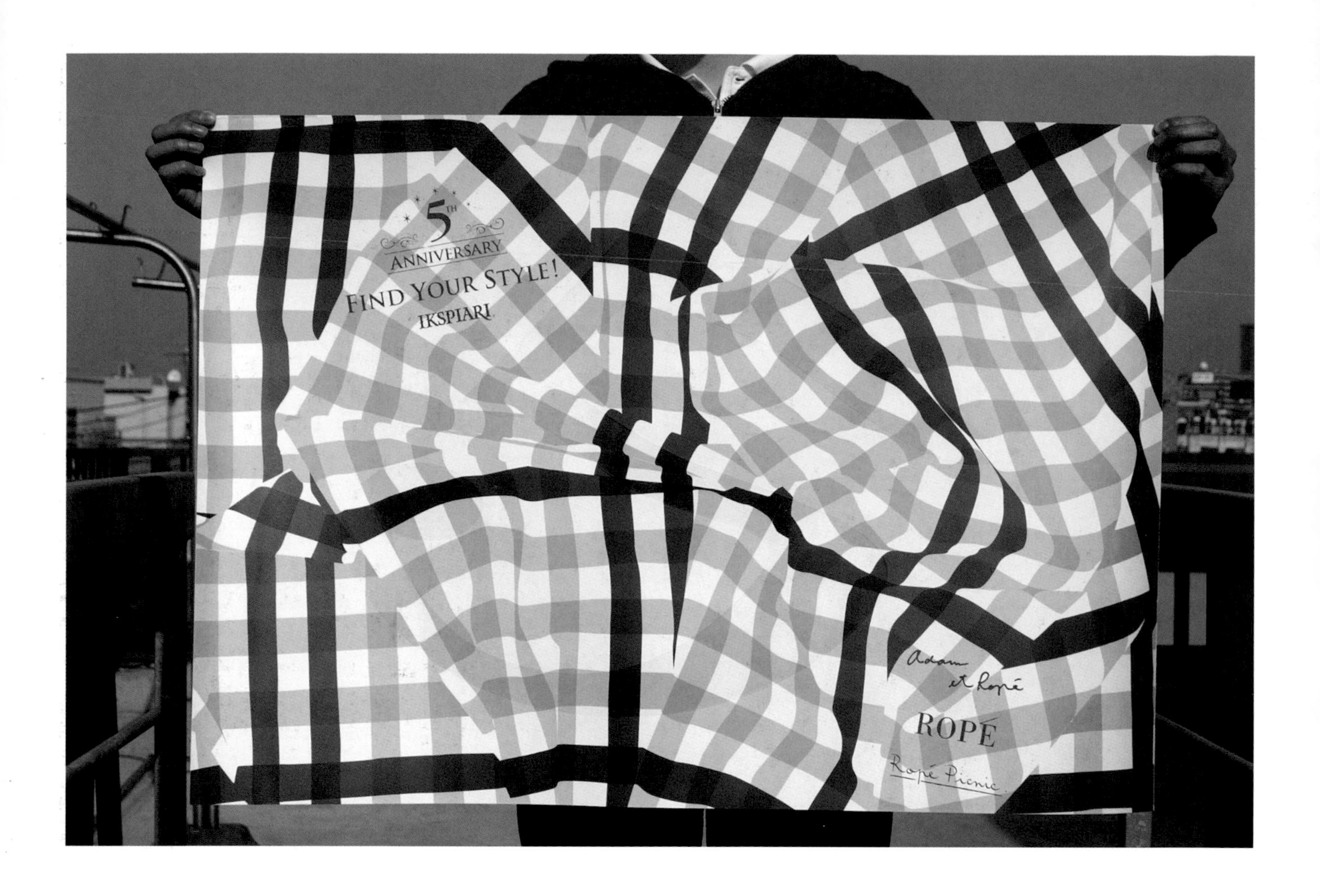

Adam et Ropé

ROPÉ

Ropé Picnic.

Bob Foundation

Tokyo, Japan

Title: - Designer: Hiromi Suzuki Client: JUN Co., Ltd. Description: The shopping bag is specially made for the 5th anniversary of a shopping mall called 'IKSPIARI' where the client's store is in. The pattern of shopping bag was originally designed for a Bob Foundation's original wrapping paper in a different colour. As it's seen the check pattern seems the 3-dimensional image on the 2-dimensional print. For designing a shopping bag, the 2-dimensional 3D image is reconstructed on the 3-dimensional surface. It's played with a visual transformation in different formats, dimensions and the character of shopping bag. The number of 5 for the anniversary is UV printed on the graphics.

ROPÉ

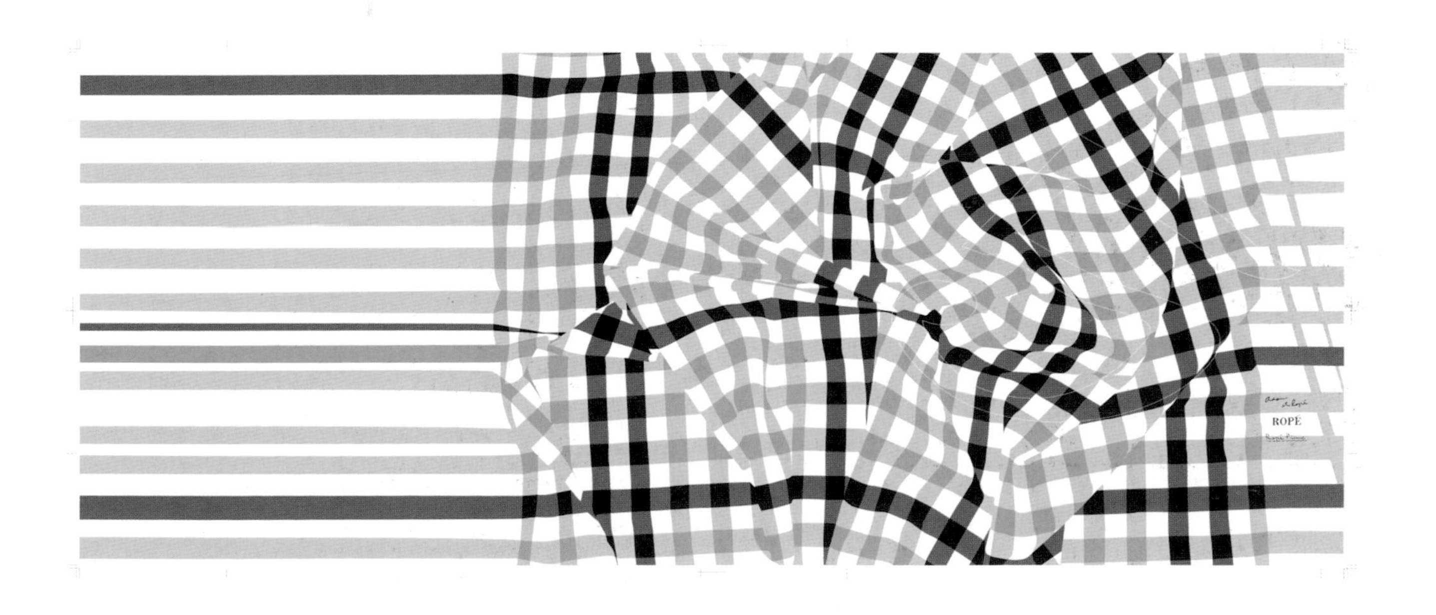
ROPÉ

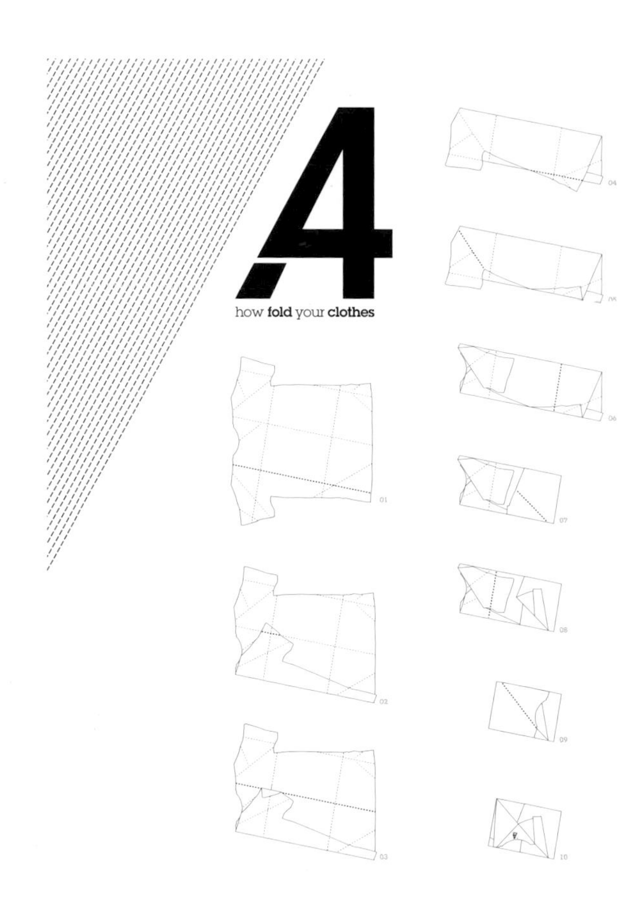

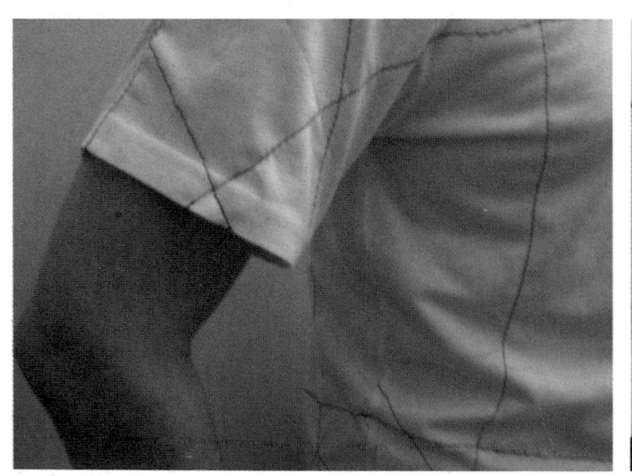

Brussels, Belgium

Title: A4 Fold your clothes Designer: kidnapyourdesigner - Caroline Dath Client: kidnapyourdesigner Description: This idea - A4 Fold your clothes - was born by turning over the pages of a book about ironing intended for the girls of the Thirties. Why not apply these concepts of folding to the design of today to the basic support, the tee shirt; and also the everyday life of the graphic designer. What could be more standard than a A4 sheet! Without counting the connection which there can be between the white of the tee and the white of a page. Meet between standard format and white product.

200g
.4
fold your clothes

.4
fold your clothes
flexible
soft
quality

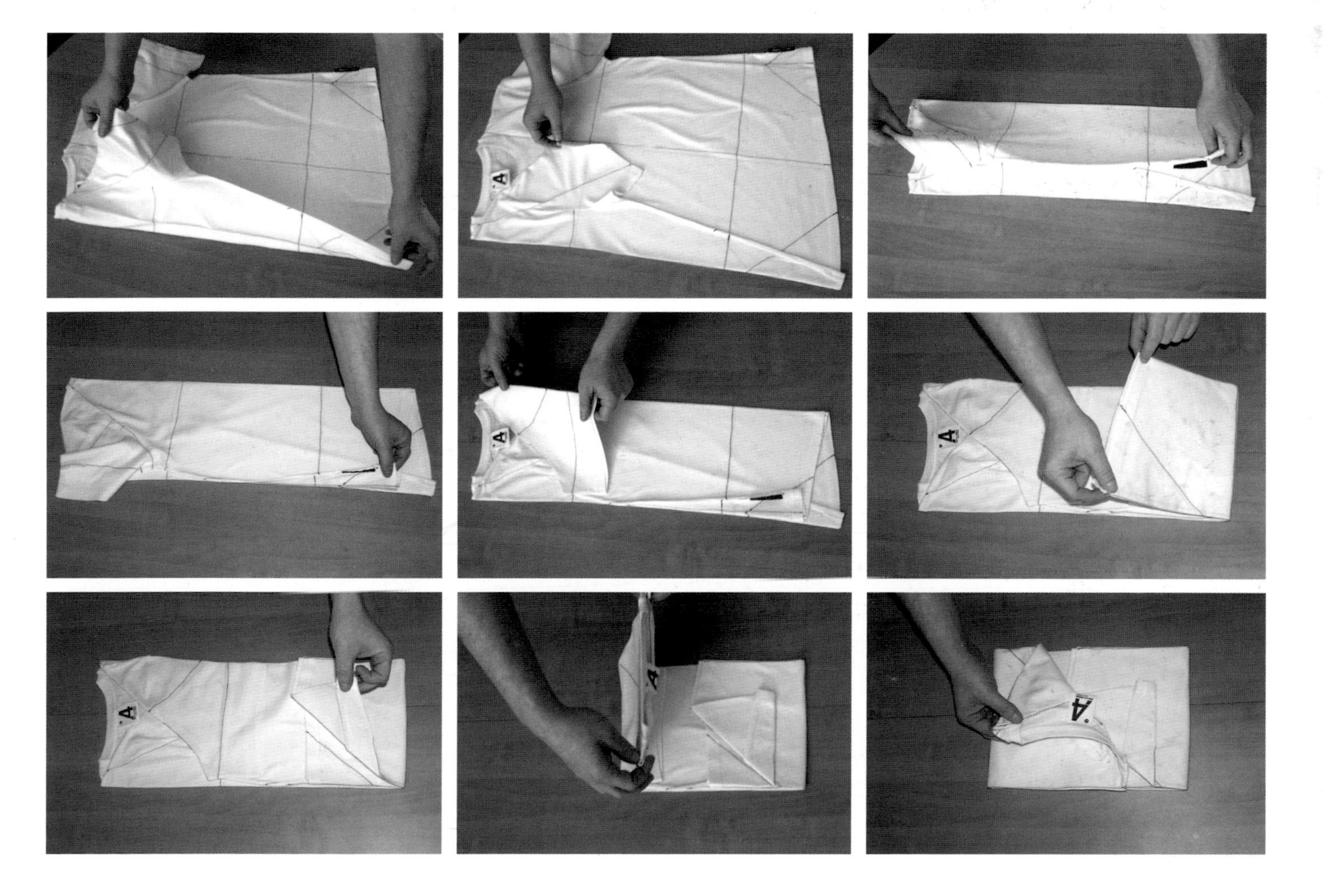

Made

Oslo, Norway

Title: NATT&DAG Designer: Made Client: NATT&DAG
Description: Made were asked to create artwork showing the nominees of the prize award, to be used as promotional material. To show the diversity of the nominees, Made used several illustrative techniques combined into a collage. The final illustration was then placed into a 'live' picture with a person holding the collage, as a metaphor for receiving an award.

2014

Berlin, Germany

Title: 'Bestiario,' Autumn/Winter 07/08 collection Designer: Nando & Silvia Photography: Hanayo, Nando Cornejo Client: potipoti Graphic Fashion Description: Bestiario, potipoti's Autumn/Winter 07/08 collection.

Henrik Vibskov

Copenhagen V, Denmark

Title: SS06 Designer: Henrik Vibskov Client: - Description: One of the most famous doctors of all time Philippus Aureolus Theophrastus Bombastus von Hohenheim - better known as Paracelsus - was part of reforming the medical world in the 15h century by using minerals in medicine. Most unfortunately he also experimented with quicksilver in his medicine whereby the expression quackery was created.

The Henrik Vibskov 'Madsen' is inspired by quack doctors and today's world selling so-called miracle cures, creating fame and great expectations.

Real or Placebo? Pull the string.

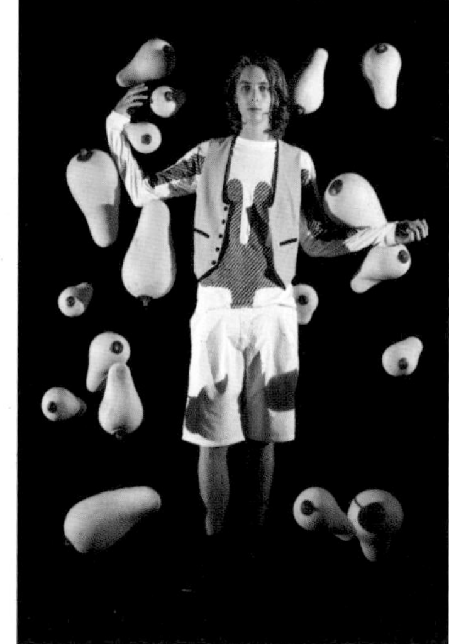

Henrik Vibskov

Copenhagen V, Denmark

Title: Big Fat Wet Shiny Boobies Collection SS07 Designer: Henrik Vibskov Client: - Description: X is the 10th collection from the Henrik Vbskov since he graduated from Central St. Martin's in 2001. The collection deals with the X (the latin 10) in prints, cuts and silhouettes. These sharp edges are contrasted with something as soft as boobs creating a sensual and humorous twist. Big fat wet shiny boobies are also be the landscape for the Paris show on July 3rd presenting a collection with jockeys, jazz, Jamaica, milk boys, soldiers, hunters, sailors and forks in and out of mind. Enjoy.

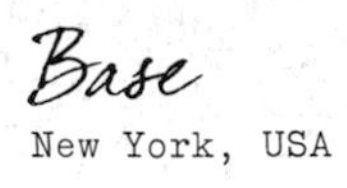

Base

New York, USA

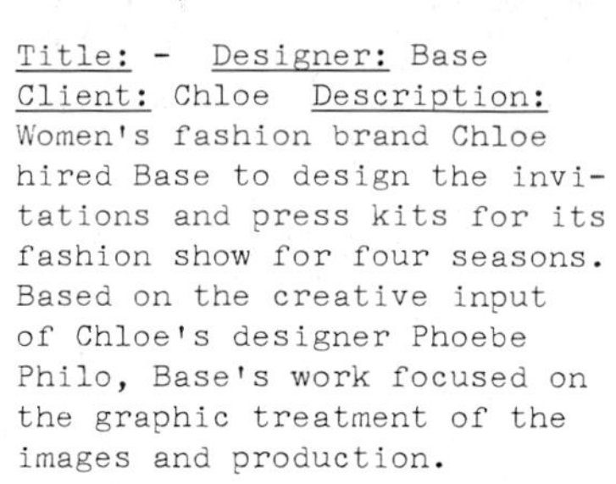

Title: - Designer: Base
Client: Chloe Description:
Women's fashion brand Chloe hired Base to design the invitations and press kits for its fashion show for four seasons. Based on the creative input of Chloe's designer Phoebe Philo, Base's work focused on the graphic treatment of the images and production.

Gold, glamorous and timeless, embodies elegance, sophistication and class. Its nature is close to those who are alluring and charming. It is also understood as a symbol for royalties and aristocrats. This splendorous mood is translated in this section of the formal wear and decoration.

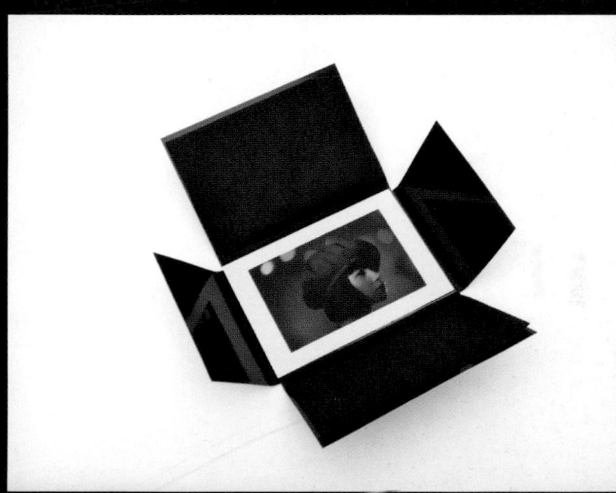

Base

New York, USA

Title: - Designer: Base Client: Maison Michel
Description: In 2006 Maison Michel, Chanel's high-end hat maker, introduced a diffusion line designed by Chanel's Accessories Designer, Laetitia Crahay. Base created the line's identity system-encompassing hang-tags, hat linings, hatboxes, and the metallic emblems adorning the hats-using a playful yet chic, type-driven graphic approach that emphasizes the word 'Chapeau!,' meaning 'Hats off!.' In addition, the studio created a press kit for Maison Michel, featuring the photographs of Serge Leblon.

HMKM

London, UK

Title: Aquascutum Advertising Designer: Colin Melia Client: Aquascutum Description: Two seasons of Aquascutum campaigns. The client brief was to create an image to engage and introduce a younger customer to the Aquascutum brand. The early campaigns stripped back the image, content to focus on the clothing, the final season introduced a narrative to the campaign in a simple clean way, so the clothing remains 'hero' in the image.

Aquascutum
LONDON

Aquascutum
LONDON

FRAGILE

Aquascutum
LONDON

London, UK

Title: - Designer: Sarah Perry
Client: Galeries Lafayette, Paris
Description: A chic and sophisticated 'signage' solution developed to signal particular product areas throughout the ground floor, without the need for words. The pictorial solution meant any visitor to the store could navigate their way around the space easily. The timeless design, using a kaleidoscope motif made up from individual products, also acts in a decorative role and maximizes the use of columns that are prevalent throughout the space. HMKM also designed the interior for ground floor accessories.

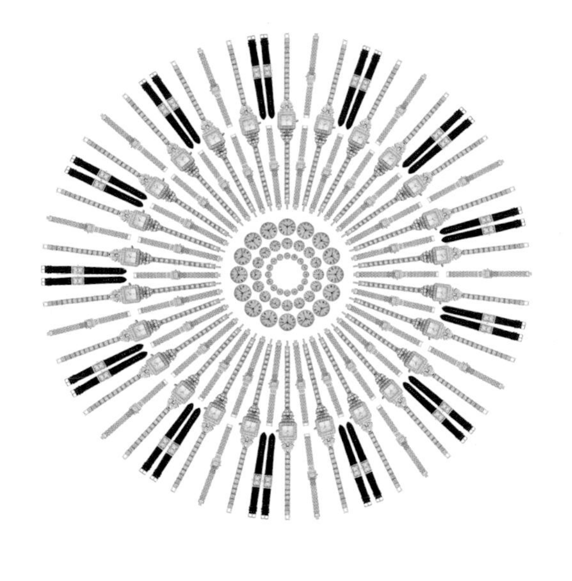

WOLFORD

GEMEY
MAYBELLINE
L'OREAL

Oslo, Norway

Title: Mette Møller Autumn collection 2007 Designer: Maria Sætre Photographer: Siren Lauvdal Client: Mette Møller/Klær uten like Description: Mette Møller is a Norwegian fashion designer who founded her brand Klær uten like in 1997. Her clothes are available in stores in Norway, Sweden and Denmark. The theme for the autumn 07 collection is the travelling carnival. Inspiration is taken from the poverty and melancholy of the 30's America. The colours are faded and dusty with elements of gold, green and black symbolizing wealth, hope and reality. Shapes are feminine, delicate and comfortable.

Høst
Autumn
07
≠

≠
Mette Møller/
Klær uten like
METTE MØLLER
Schleppegrellsgate 26
NO-0556 Oslo, Norway
tel: +47 95 03 14 61
fax: +47 22 35 14 33
mette@mettemoller.no
www.mettemoller.no
DESIGNERS AGENTS
Skovveien 7
NO-0257 Oslo, Norway
tel: +47 93 48 90 87
fax: +47 22 44 95 24
connie@designersagents.com
www.designersagents.com
ONLINE SHOP
www.mettemoller.no

Scandinavian DesignLab
Copenhagen K, Denmark

Title: 'Graphics in Fashion' Exhibition Designer: Dyhr.Hagen, Scandinavian DesignLab, 2GD Client: - Description: In occasion of the Copenhagen Fashion Week the design agencies Scandinavian DesignLab, Dyhr.Hagen and Gold Studio presents the exhibition 'Graphics In Fashion'. An idea developed from the international success and interest received by the Danish fashion industry. The purpose is to show how designers work with graphic solutions within fashion, and to visualize extra dimension that can be added whether it's talking about clothes, furniture or other fashion related products. This exhibition is an example on how product campaigns and marketing communication over time merges together with the latest development and trends in graphic design.

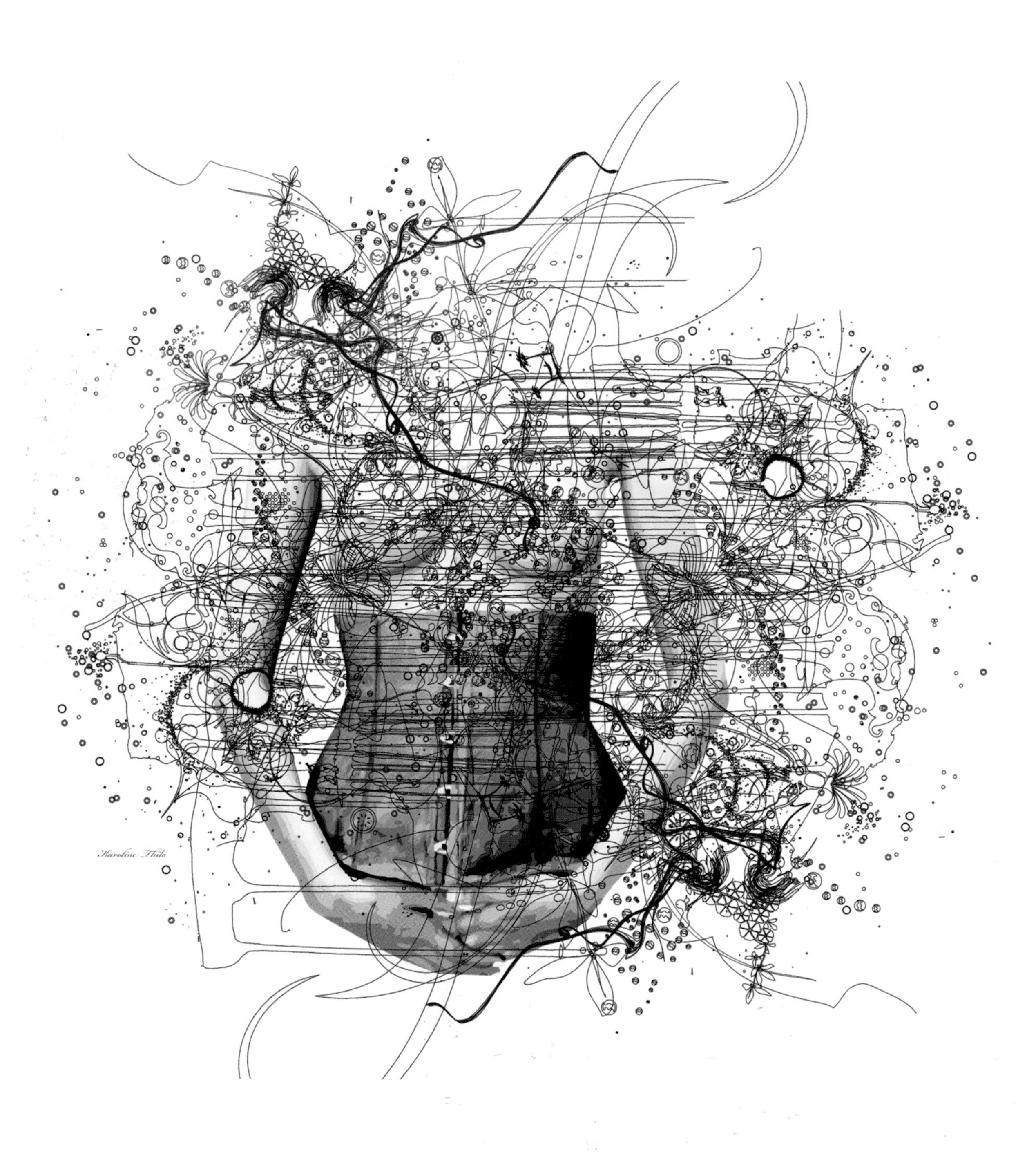
Karoline Thilo

COLLECTION
SS2006
GRAPHICS IN
FASHION

Plazm Media, Inc.

Oregon, Portland

Title: Jantzen Brandbook Designer: Joshua Berger, Niko Courtelis, Enrique Mosqueda, Pete McCracken Client: Jantzen Swimwear Description: Based on research supplied by Jantzen, Plazm's objective was to redirect the marketing to a younger demographic, to develop the next generation of Jantzen customers, to nurture downstream business, and to build future advocacy. The perception of the brand was 'old' - suits your grandmother would wear.

jantzen
.01

Saturday London

London, UK

Title: J.Lindeberg Spring Summer 2007 Designer: Saturday Photographer: Andreas Larson Client: J.Lindeberg Description: Rather than the usual lookbook format, Saturday decided to capture the attention of the readers and created a story. Teaming up with the International fashion photographer Andreas Larson Saturday shot an editorially led set of images, mixing studio with street locations and colour with black and white. There is a strong sense of tempo to highlight the different moods of the collection. The shoot was then compiled into a sizeable look-book with a copper foiled cover.

02
Shirt Noreen Day Gorgette / Shorts Joan Ultimate Com Blue / Jacket Yasmine Ultimate Com Blue

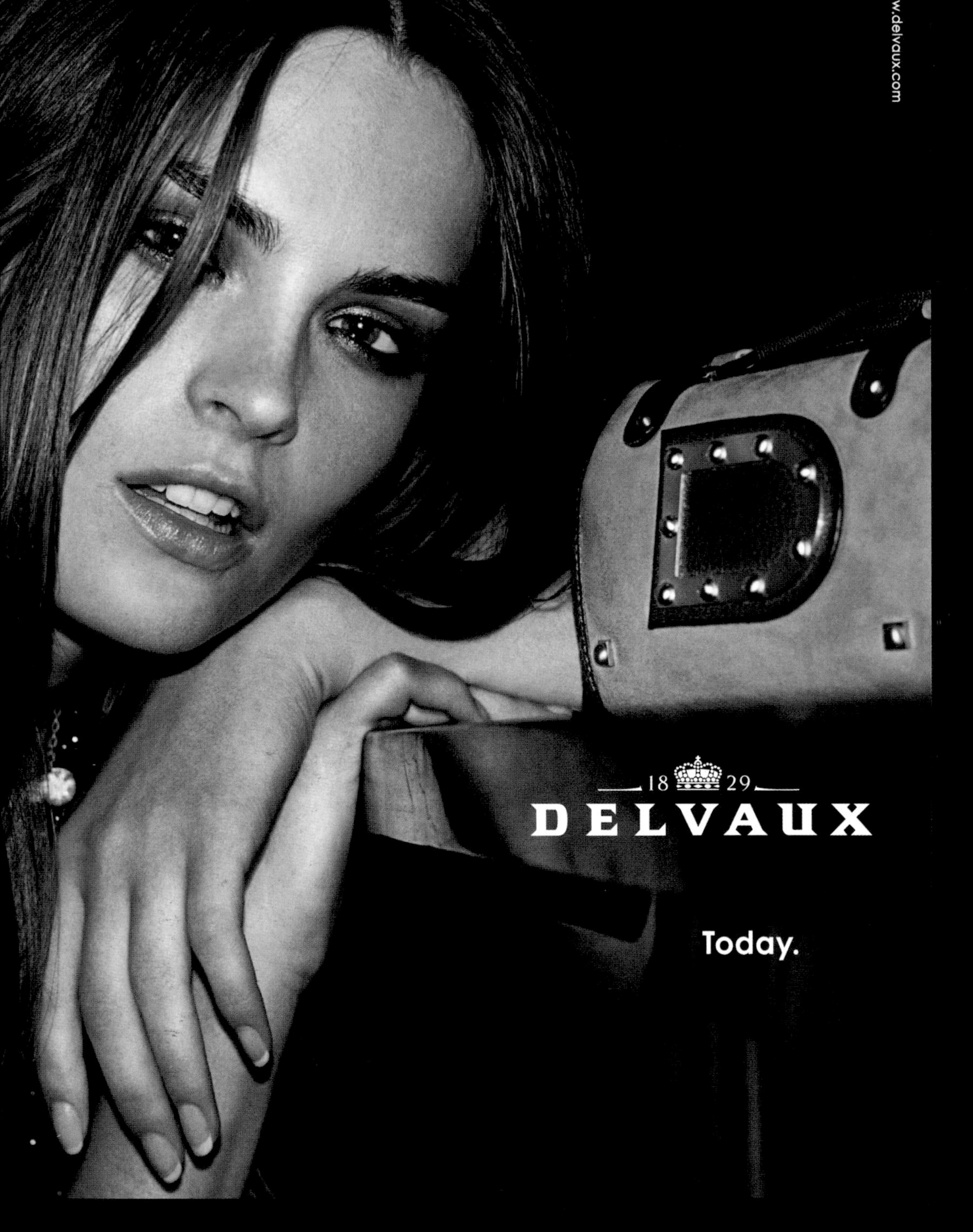

New York, USA

Title: - Designer: Base Client: Delvaux Description: In 2004 Delvaux, the Europe's oldest accessories and leather-goods company, celebrated its 175th anniversary. In conjunction with this landmark Base conceived, designed, and produced a commemorative book. Base asked 175 artists (photographers, stylists, designers, painters, writers, etc.) to create a page each, based on a different Delvaux-related item. Base also art directed and developed a series of ad campaigns for Delvaux, establishing top Belgian model Anouk Lepere as the face of Delvaux. To convey the line's modernity, the studio incorporated the word 'Today' in conjunction with the images.

www.delvaux.com
18 29
DELVAUX
Today.

18 29
DELVAUX
Today.

www.delvaux.com
18 29
DELVAUX
Today.

*　　**

***

Anja Kroencke (TRAFFIC Creative Management)

New York, USA

* Title: Face of Desire ** Title: Nude with Birds
*** Title: Floating Sisters

Designer: Anita Mrusek Client: Squint Magazine Description: The above are from a series of 6 called 'Wings of Desire.' The theme was 'New Romance' and the designer tried to create a modern day version of Marie Antoinette.

**** Title: Anja's Poppy ***** Title: Bloomed
****** Title: Beauty

Designer: - Client: Squint Magazine Description: The above are from a series of 4 called 'Poppy Dreams.'

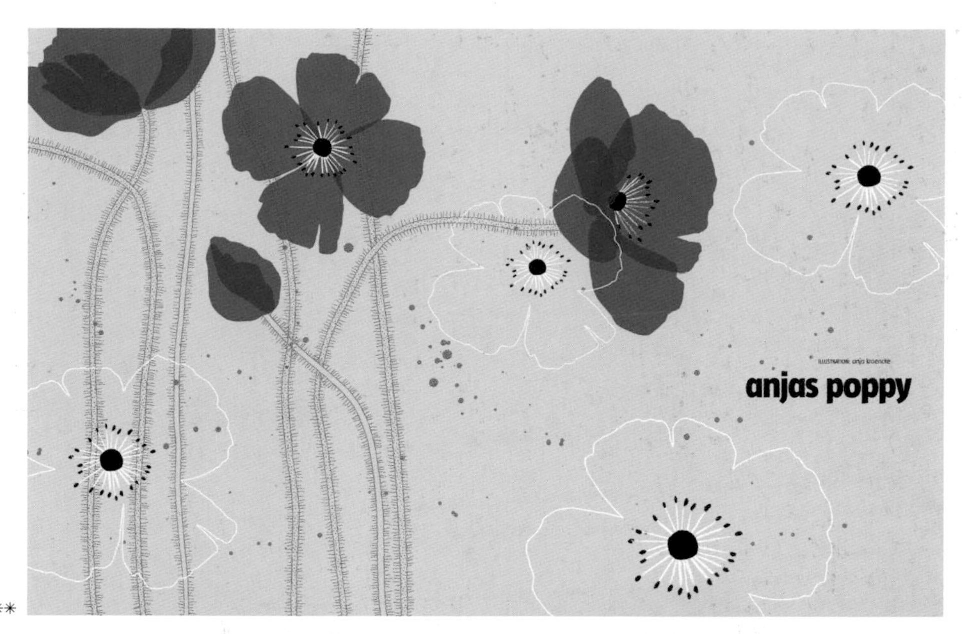
anjas poppy

****

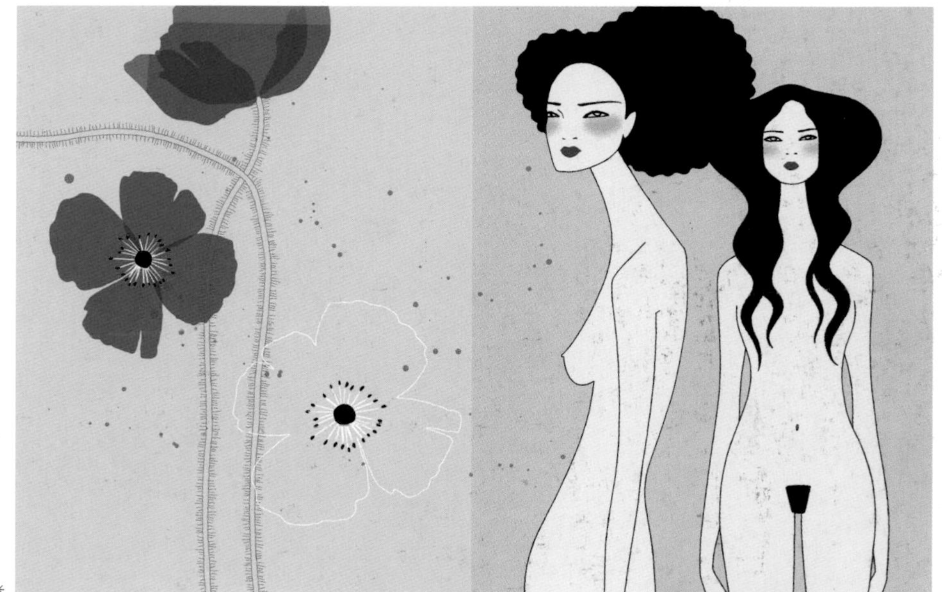

*****

******

Deanne Cheuk Design

New York, USA

Title: Sue Stemp Illustrations
Designer: Deanne Cheuk Client: Sue Stemp Description: Illustrations for the Sue Stemp Spring/Fall 2006, and 2007 Collections. Invitation and hangtag for the Spring 2007 Collection. The Spring 2007 Collection was titled 'Byrd of America,' and Fall 2006 was called 'Honeymoon Delight.' Sue Stemp's distinct personal style reflects in her fashion designs, bringing together relaxed, feminine silhouettes with sharp English tailoring and a flirty, modern, cool.

Deanne Cheuk Design

New York, USA

Title: Sue Stemp Illustrations
Designer: Deanne Cheuk Client: Sue Stemp Description: Illustrations for the Sue Stemp Spring/Fall 2006, and 2007 Collections. Invitation and hangtag for the Spring 2007 Collection.

sue stemp

Surface to air. Paris

Paris, France

Title: - Designer: Santiago Marotto, Jeremie Rozan Photographer: Viviane Sassen Client: Tsumori Chisato SS 07 Description: Tsumori Chisato always create a universe based on feminity and magic, the surrealism and the beauty. The challenge every season is to get these elements in a new proposition.

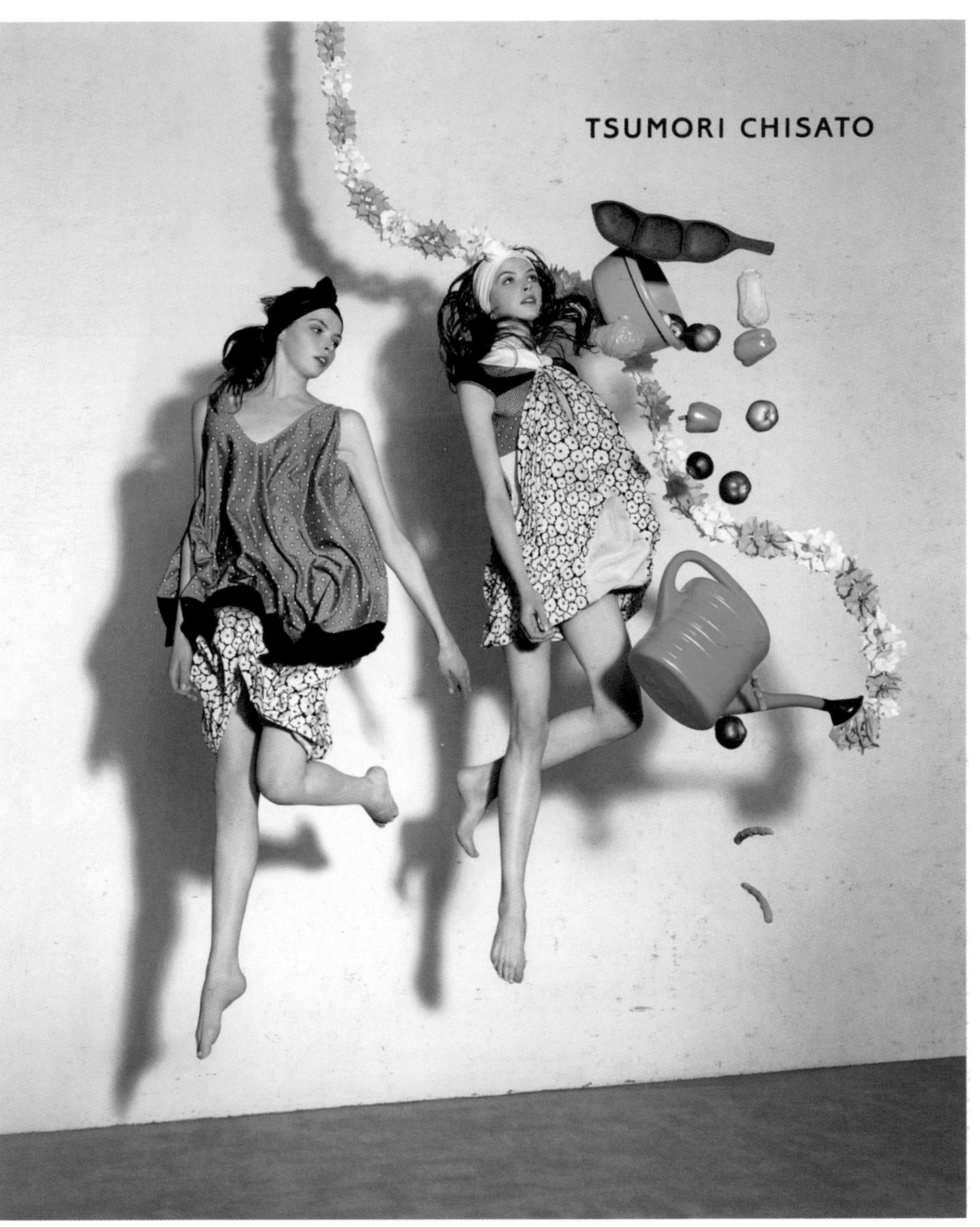
TSUMORI CHISATO

TSUMORI CHISATO

TSUMORI CHISATO

Stockholm, Sweden

Title: Prefab Designer: Johan Hjerpe Photographer: Philip Karlberg Client: Diana Orving Description: In-store posters, 50x70cm Lambda prints. For a collection made out of cheap, modified garments from other brands.

Atomic Attack!

Hong Kong, China

Title: Red Earth Metro Glamour cosmetic line Designer: Calvin Ho Client: Red Earth Hong Kong, Red Earth UK Description: Red Earth needed something really 'out there' compared with their usual marketing and branding. They wanted something hip and cityscape to align with their product 'Metro Glamour.' City life is forever in motion, with multi layers hence the design reflects this. This was originally designed for a PR pack in a DVD format for magazines, and Red Earth liked it so much it decided to put it in the store on a big widescreen TV in the London Store as well.

Madrid, Spain

Title: - Designer: Carmen Garcia Huerta Client: Eric Bompard Description: Advertising campaign for French cashmere garments ERIC BOMPARD. Huerta has been developing these campaigns for three consecutive years (2004-2006). The main character is always a chic and sophisticated goat.

Carmen Garcia Huerta

Madrid, Spain

Title: - Designer: Carmen Garcia Huerta Client: VOGUE Spain Description: Different samples of Huerta's work for Spanish VOGUE, along two years.

Dior
Dior
Dior
Dior

*

Carmen Garcia Huerta

Madrid, Spain

* Title: 'A monster that gobbles up it all'

** Title: 'Aggressive and rebel women'

Designer: Carmen Garcia Huerta Client: El Pais Semanal Description: Every season the magazine El Pais Semanal launches a special issue on fashion. Normally Huerta is the one who illustrates it.

**

Boredomsqueezer
Hong Kong, China

Title: Walking Paradise Designer: Alice Mok, Regina Ho Client: - Description: 'WALKING PARADISE' with the idea of bringing people a unique and fresh feeling about action figure. Its theme should not be limited to military, science or cartoon, but also with fashionable elements to show the latest trend. The designers make the action figure in new phase, with most trendy costume to show its uniqueness - it is neither the display nor plaything, but a media to show lifestyle.

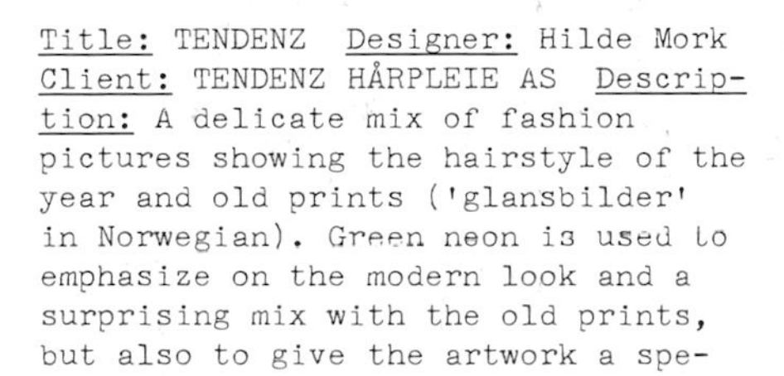

Commando Group
Oslo, Norway

Title: TENDENZ Designer: Hilde Mork Client: TENDENZ HÅRPLEIE AS Description: A delicate mix of fashion pictures showing the hairstyle of the year and old prints ('glansbilder' in Norwegian). Green neon is used to emphasize on the modern look and a surprising mix with the old prints, but also to give the artwork a special finish.

Fedoralime AMFC

New York, USA

Title: G-Unit Clothing Company Campaign Spring 2005 Designer: Romeo Tajhal Photographer: Zach Gold Client: G-Unit Clothing Company / Marc Ecko Enterprises Description: Seasonal Fashion campaign 'Choppers and Cream.' Inspired by movies like 'The Wild One' and 'Easy Rider.' The campaign depicts a fictional ice cream parlor that also acts as a motorcycle club. The G-Unit bikers club storms into town after a big score. While fueling up their bikes they enjoy the company of the local females.

G Unit
CLOTHING COMPANY
G-unit
shop online at g-unitclothing.com
RY OPPORTUNITY.
E BROTHERHOOD.

Base

New York, USA

Title: - Designer: Base Client: Chloe Description: Women's fashion brand Chloe hired Base to design the invitations and press kits for its fashion show for four seasons. Based on the creative input of Chloe's designer Phoebe Philo, Base's work focused on the graphic treatment of the images and production.

MATERIALBYPRODUCT

Victoria, Australia

Title: Soft Hard Harder 0708 Designer: Chantal McDonald, Susan Dimasi Photographer: Paul Knight, Justin Edward John Smith Client: MATERIALBYPRODUCT Description: The concept behind the 'Hero Shots' is in the meeting of Fashion and Fine Art photography. Produced as a pair of double sided posters; one side printed in full colour with a high gloss finish, the other in black and white with a matt finish that feature key garments from the seasonal fashion collections of MATERIALBYPODUCT. The approach to the creation of these images is in the spirit of true collaboration, where MATERIALBYPODUCT delivers garments to the photographer, who then places them in the context of their own work. Similar to the garments, the image is not prescribed by a theme.

MATERIALBY-PRODUCT

Victoria, Australia

* Title: Soft Hard Harder 0708, 'Hero Shots' Designer: Chantal McDonald, Susan Dimasi Photographer: Paul Knight Client: MATERIALBYPRODUCT

** Title: Soft Hard 07, MATERIALBYPRODUCT in Paris Designer: Chantal McDonald, Susan Dimasi Client: MATERIALBY-PRODUCT Description: Reusing the 'Hero Shots' created for the MATERIALBYPRODUCT promotional posters, these invitations were designed for the Spring/Summer 07 collection, aiming to intrigue the viewer via the image.

SOFT HARD 07 / **Material By Product**
Available for appointments / 24 September – 10 October 2006
Tel: +61 433 944 864 / info@materialbyproduct.com

Art Direction & Design / 3 Deep Design / www.3deep.com.au / Image / Paul Knight

**

SOFT HARD 07 / Material By Product
Available for appointments / 24 September – 10 October 2006
Tel: +61 433 944 864 / info@materialbyproduct.com

**

*** Title: Soft Hard Harder 0708, MATERIALBYPRODUCT at Redez-Vous Designer: David Roennfeldt Client: MATERIALBY-PRODUCT Description: An invitation designed in conjunction with a series of four photographic images for the Autumn/Winter 07/08 collection.

Material by Product
SOFT HARD HARDER 07/08 AW

Rendez-vous Femme 1-4 Mars 07
67 Rue du Faubourg,
Saint Martin, 75010 Paris,
&
85-87 Rue du Faubourg,
Saint Martin, 75010 Paris

By appointment 5-10 Mars 07
Telephone +61 (0)433 944 864

Press Agent: www.agenturv.de

www.materialbyproduct.com
info@materialbyproduct.com

***

*

SOFT HARD 07 / **Material By Product**
Available for appointments / 24 September – 10 October 2006
Tel: +61 433 944 864 / info@materialbyproduct.com

Art Direction & Design / 3 Deep Design / www.3deep.com.au / Image / Justin Edward John Smith

MATERIALBYPRODUCT

Victoria, Australia

Title: 'In-House' show, Soft Hard 07 Designer: Chantal McDonald, Susan Dimasi Client: MATERIALBYPRODUCT Description: The concept behind the 'In-House' show is a simple but striking opening up of the studio doors, through which we present our fashion collections at the completion of each collection. The format of the show collapses the back and front stage of the standard catwalk, with the dressing and undressing of a model being just as visible as the 'walk' itself. It celebrates the ceremony of dressing, and slows down fast paced fashion.

12 14 16
15
18
20

New York, USA

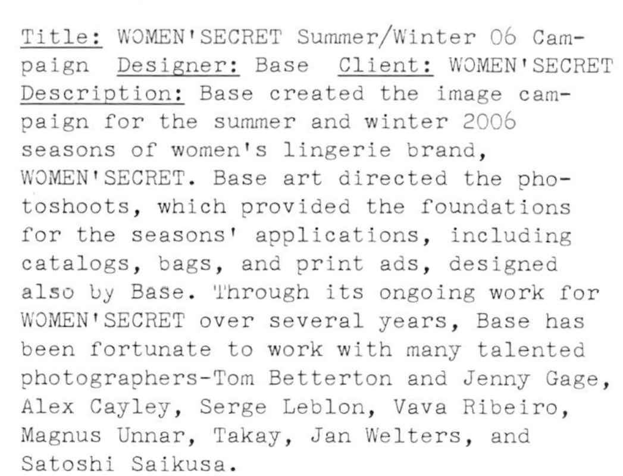

Title: WOMEN'SECRET Summer/Winter 06 Campaign Designer: Base Client: WOMEN'SECRET Description: Base created the image campaign for the summer and winter 2006 seasons of women's lingerie brand, WOMEN'SECRET. Base art directed the photoshoots, which provided the foundations for the seasons' applications, including catalogs, bags, and print ads, designed also by Base. Through its ongoing work for WOMEN'SECRET over several years, Base has been fortunate to work with many talented photographers-Tom Betterton and Jenny Gage, Alex Cayley, Serge Leblon, Vava Ribeiro, Magnus Unnar, Takay, Jan Welters, and Satoshi Saikusa.

Base

New York, USA

Title: WOMEN'SECRET Summer/Winter 06 Campaign Designer: Base Client: WOMEN'SECRET Description: Base created the image campaign for the summer and winter 2006 seasons of women's lingerie brand, WOMEN'SECRET. Base art directed the photoshoots, which provided the foundations for the seasons' applications, including catalogs, bags, and print ads, designed also by Base. Through its ongoing work for WOMEN'SECRET over several years, Base has been fortunate to work with many talented photographers-Tom Betterton and Jenny Gage, Alex Cayley, Serge Leblon, Vava Ribeiro, Magnus Unnar, Takay, Jan Welters, and Satoshi Saikusa.

Saturday London
London, UK

Title: Hogan Designer: Saturday Photographer: Phil Poynter from Mona Johanson Client: Hogan Description: The Italian luxury goods company came to Saturday to art direct their advertising campaign. Saturday created the notion of a European lifestyle, a snapshot of the best 5% of your life, recreated in front of the camera. The S/S campaign was shot on location in Miami.

Black, the mystery colour of all, is intense but surprising, melancholic but romantic. It lives in the dark worlds of circus and underworld, far far away where clowns, magic and spirits take shelter. This section brings you to the sinister side of fashion where nothing is what it seems.

BLACK

Serum Vs Venom / SVSV

New York, USA

Title: aformofwar Designer: Jenna Rivers, David Gensler, Aerosyn-Lex Photographer: Kareem Black Client: The KDU / Serum Versus Venom Description: At the time of this collection, the designer were living in a steady fear of terrorism, so they focused on materials and designs that took into consideration issues of safety. The extreme utility was also a reaction to their first collection, which focused on lush natural fibers, which at this time seemed excessive.

ALIEN

GHOS

Atomic Attack!

Hong Kong, China

Title: Role Play Designer: Calvin Ho Client: Hint Magazine New York Description: The designer thought about woman's role in society and their personalities. What that person is and what they dream of becoming. From this the designer put the model into their respective environments. He deliberately chose nature scenes as it somehow contrasted nicely with the styling - the mountains and forest forced the idea of dreamlike innocence and childhood. He was also trying to see how our environment molds us or whether we blend in. It gave this whole shoot a sense of natural purity. Atomic Attack! also added a twist and put them into funny or sad situations with illustrations on top. The indecisive woman getting stuck between two mountains - to a girl that refuses to grow up. It is hopefully quite obvious to the viewer and it is not meant to be totally serious, much like fashion and its power of roleplay. This is fully animated using flash.

MASOCHIST

Atomic Attack!

Hong Kong, China

Title: Role Play Designer: Calvin Ho Client: Hint Magazine New York Description: The designer thought about woman's role in society and their personalities. What that person is and what they dream of becoming. From this the designer put the model into their respective environments. He deliberately chose nature scenes as it somehow contrasted nicely with the styling - the mountains and forest forced the idea of dreamlike innocence and childhood. He was also trying to see how our environment molds us or whether we blend in. It gave this whole shoot a sense of natural purity. Atomic Attack! also added a twist and put them into funny or sad situations with illustrations on top. The indecisive woman getting stuck between two mountains - to a girl that refuses to grow up. It is hopefully quite obvious to the viewer and it is not meant to be totally serious, much like fashion and its power of role-play. This is fully animated using flash.

Atomic Attack!

Hong Kong, China

Title: Noir East Designer: Calvin Ho Client: Hint Magazine New York Description: Atomic Attack! first project with Hint Magazine. The photos were originally in plain background and colours were very different. The designer cut the figures out, put them into a Japanese painting like environment, and re-edited them as creatures of the night. The concept was inspired by classic horror films and early Andy Warhol films, Jean Cocteau's Surreal Orpheus Trilogy. He loves old Japanese paintings and it was a great chance to create beautiful horrific creatures. It almost feels like a high-class b-grade movie if there is ever such a thing. The most interesting challenge is that after the photos were taken they were then given to Atomic Attack! with absolutely no background or communication. So the end result is the personal reaction of the designer to ingredients provided by another creative group, which is really interesting. This is fully animated using flash.

Atomic Attack!

Hong Kong, China

Title: Noir East Designer: Calvin Ho Client: Hint Magazine New York Description: Atomic Attack! first project with Hint Magazine. The photos were originally in plain background and colours were very different. The designer cut the figures out, put them into a Japanese painting like environment, and re-edited them as creatures of the night. The concept was inspired by classic horror films and early Andy Warhol films, Jean Cocteau's Surreal Orpheus Trilogy. He loves old Japanese paintings and it was a great chance to create beautiful horrific creatures. It almost feels like a high-class b-grade movie if there is ever such a thing. The most interesting challenge is that after the photos were taken they were then given to Atomic Attack! with absolutely no background or communication. So the end result is the personal reaction of the designer to ingredients provided by another creative group, which is really interesting. This is fully animated using flash.

Dzark Designbureau

Clifton, USA

Title: - Designer: Nedjelco-Michel Karlovich, Virgilio Santos Photographer: Nicholas Routzen Client: Nicholas Routzen Description: It is a fashion series by Brooklyn photographer Nicholas Routzen for a private client.

The big Money game TM

lo Mr. Monster
elcome to the eve of destruction

Hong Kong, China

Title: Black Magick Designer: Hei, Beardsley Photographer: Hei Client: City Magazine, Green Studio Description: This woman has very dynamic posture and she has some sort of mysterious look in her, designers were listening to a sound named Black Magic Woman by Santana while working on this photo, guess they got this influence.

Hong Kong, China

Title: Forest Designer: Hei, Beardsley Photographer: Hei Client: Private I, Green Studio Description: Like some folk tales, there are many fairies that live in the forest.

LB

In my imagination..... behind every necklace under every frock there lives a woman....
take her frock off..... leave her necklace..... let her keep her bag,
and her hat on......
allow me to present Mimco's summer 05 accessories collection.....
"Blurring the lines"

I hope you enjoy "blurring the lines" as much as i've enjoyed imagining, creating & designing it.
Endless gratitude to mimi and Dandi's precious team

My deepest heartfelt appreciation to the exceptional women who have made this parade possible
Rachelle Dendle
Kathryn Baulch
Jessica Frid
Nicole Edwards

I have to thank from the bottom of my heart, Grant for unconditional support and invaluable wisdom.
Jarrad for scoping and (patiently) explaining.
Donni (ku de ta) for magical music.
Linda Britten for superb lingerie suits
Rebecca Wetzler for incredible illustration
Mac for fantastic faces.

Amanda

ps. are accessories fashion??

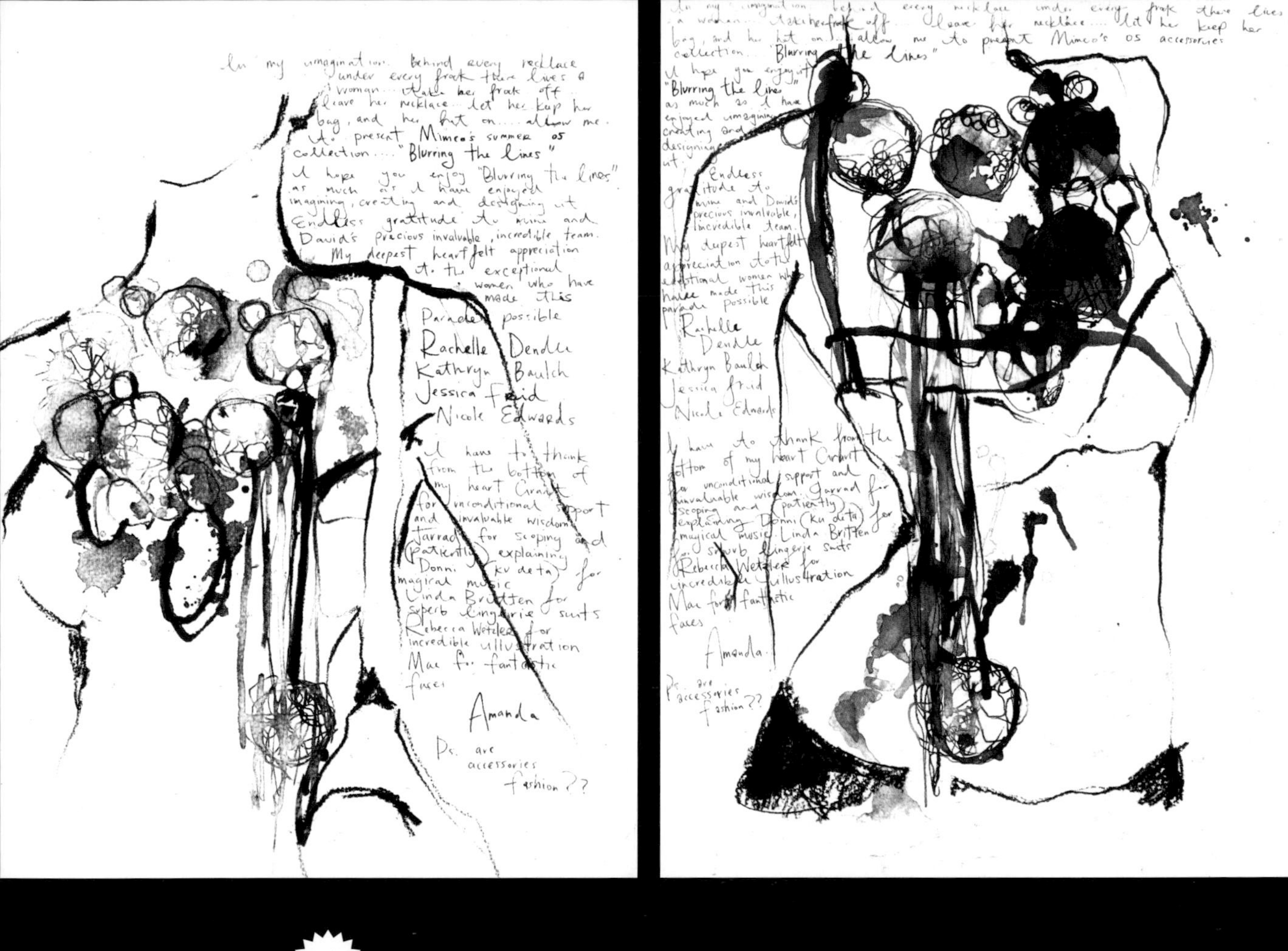

Sydney, Australia

Title: Programs for Sydney fashion week 2005 Designer: Rebecca Wetzler Client: mimco Description: It is a mix media design for a program of Mimco's show at Sydney fashion week. A series of 3 illustrations with hand lettering is produced, done in ink and charcoal. Printed on thick watercolour paper.

Stockholm, Sweden

Title: Orlando Autumn/Winter 2005 Designer: Johan Hjerpe Photographer: Daniel Skoog Client: Diana Orving Description: Images for a collection based on the book Orlando by Virginia Woolf. The collection emphasises on Orlando's shift from man to woman during the book, by incorporating changeable garments. It also picks up on codes and mixes meanings and rules from the several hundred years of the life of the main character. The mix continues in the graphical symbols in the photography.

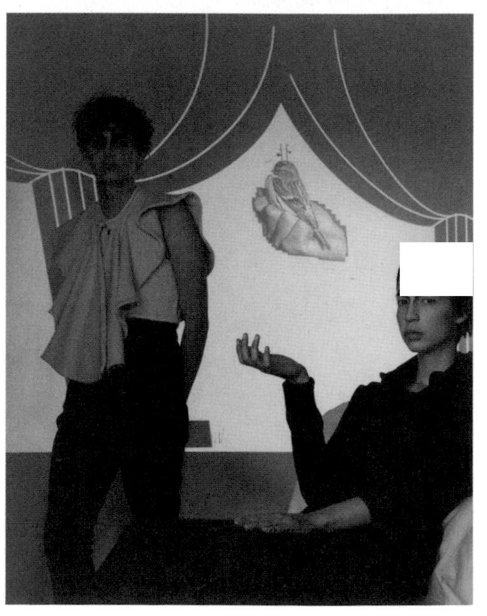

Yke Schotten (Unit CMA)

Rotterdam, The Netherlands

Title: Impromptu Designer: Yke Schotten Photographer: Klaas Jan Kliphuis Client: Blvd Magazine Description: Photography and illustration combined in images for fashion editorial in Blvd magazine. Theme 'black & white.'

*

**

***

Amelie Hegardt (TRAFFIC Creative Management)

New York, USA

* Title: D&G Designer: Amelie Hegardt Client: Holt Renfrew Description: Illustration for a catalogue text featuring Dolce and Gabbana, and their inspiration from the Italian countryside.

** Title: Bohème Designer: Nassoud Mansouri Client: Godiva Description: An illustration for Bohème, inspired by the power of free women. It has a spiritual, feminine and strong character.

*** Title: Armani Designer: Amelie Hegardt Client: Blackbook Description: One of six illustrations published in Blackbook September 2005, covering high-end brands such as Armani and Ralph Lauren. The dress was inspired by one of Armani's dresses.

*****

****

**** Title: Texture Designer: Saturday London Client: Umberto Gianini Description: Illustrations made for Umberto Gianninis hair products which is used for protecting the hair from pollution and environmental damages.

***** Title: GRAVITY Designer: Amelie Hegardt Client: - Description: Unpublished. Originally inspired by a fashion story. Innocent sensuality.

James Dignan (Unit CMA & Art Liaison)

Sydney, Australia

<u>Title:</u> 'Artworks' <u>Designer:</u> Eric Matthews
<u>Client:</u> Autore South Sea Pearls (Australia)
<u>Description:</u> Editorial Fashion series combing outfits from the Paris Haute Couture collections with jewellery from the Autore South Sea Pearls collection for their magazine 'Autore.'

GIVENCHY
THE LATE AUDREY HEPBURN REMAINS AN ICONIC MUSE FOR THE FASHION HOUSE. MANY WOMEN WISH THEY COULD LOOK LIKE HER, AND IF DESIGNER JULIEN MACDONALD HAS HIS WAY, THEY WILL. 18CT WHITE GOLD PENDANT, FEATURING PAVE-SET DIAMONDS, A BRILLIANT CUT GARNET AND WHITE AUTORE SOUTH SEA PEARL.

PHILIP TREACY
FEATHERS WERE THE NEAREST THING TO CONVENTIONAL HEADGEAR AT THE HAT DESIGNER'S SPRING-SUMMER SHOW, WHICH ALSO FEATURED NAOMI CAMPBELL WEARING A CAN OF CAMPBELL'S SOUP ON HER HEAD. CHOKER OF ROUND WHITE AUTORE SOUTH SEA PEARLS.

EMANUEL UNGARO
THE 70-YEAR-OLD DESIGNER REFUSES TO RETIRE UNTIL HE ANSWERS THE QUESTION, "WHAT DO WOMEN WANT?" WE SAY RETIRE IN PEACE - YOU'D BE CRAZY NOT TO WANT HIS SLINKY, SENSUAL GOWN THAT SPELLS TEMPTATION. 18CT WHITE AND YELLOW GOLD DIAMOND NECKLET WITH 10 (NOT ALL SHOWN) WHITE AUTORE SOUTH SEA PEARLS.

JEAN PAUL GAULTIER
CLASSIC ELEGANCE AND SUPERB TAILORING DISPLAY GAULTIER'S LOVE OF HAUTE COUTURE. THIS IS A GOWN WORTHY OF A BEST ACTRESS – NICOLE KIDMAN WORE IT TO THIS YEAR'S ACADEMY AWARDS. 18CT WHITE AND YELLOW GOLD DIAMOND SET NECKLET WITH EIGHT (NOT ALL SHOWN) GOLD AUTORE SOUTH SEA PEARLS.

Bleed

Oslo, Norway

Title: Leave Your Mark Designer: Kjetil Wold, Erik Hedberg Client: Alu Spa
Description: The LEAVE YOUR MARK concept is street art meeting high-end fashion, focuses on the personalization on how different people leave their mark and how this is adapted in the fashion industry. Stencil art and handwriting on top of renderings. A sexy mix of photography and illustration, the LEAVE YOUR MARK subject runs thru the book with different levels of metaphors and design solutions. The catalogue has pre-printed a set of sticky notes so the user can mark their favorite pages. The street-art scene inspired a lot but also the way international fashion brands use patterns and repetitions to create a visual experience. Mixing these two worlds was the main idea behind.

ALU
LEAVE YOUR MARK
Tarolo
Quadro
Wall
Frame
Acrobat
Acrobat Slim
Reed
Pylon
Stylo
Autopole
Box

MO BEARDSLEY

**

**

Hong Kong, China

* Title: Romantic Designer: Hei, Beardsley Photographer: Hei Client: Store Magazine, Green Studio Description: Being a creative duo - photographer and illustrator, the designers hope to create some work with both their profession, so it is like a wedding of photography and illustration.

Usually Green Studio sees invisible and possible images from a photograph and then illustrates or adds images on it spontaneously.

This photograph reminds the designers of backstage circus, therefore they add in some circus elements.

** Title: - Designer: Hei, Beardsley Photographer: Hei Client: Il Colpo, Green Studio Description: Designers want to depict lonely souls in the city.

Vault49 LLC

New York, USA

Title: The Greatest Show On Earth Designer: John Glasgow, Jonathan Kenyon, Daryl Waller, Si Scott Photographer: Vault49 Client: Style Montecarlo Magazine Description: The Greatest Show On Earth is inspired by a world of questionable morality and alternative pastimes, influenced by the lives and performances of early twentieth century traveling entertainers. Worlds collide to give birth to a fresh collection of unforgettable images ranging from the sublime to the fanciful.

With advance fashion collections from various designers and props from around the world, this shoot is in-keeping with the collaborative spirit in which Vault49 was conceived, The Greatest Show On Earth showcases Vault49's partnership with some of the hottest photographic, illustrative and typographic talent around.

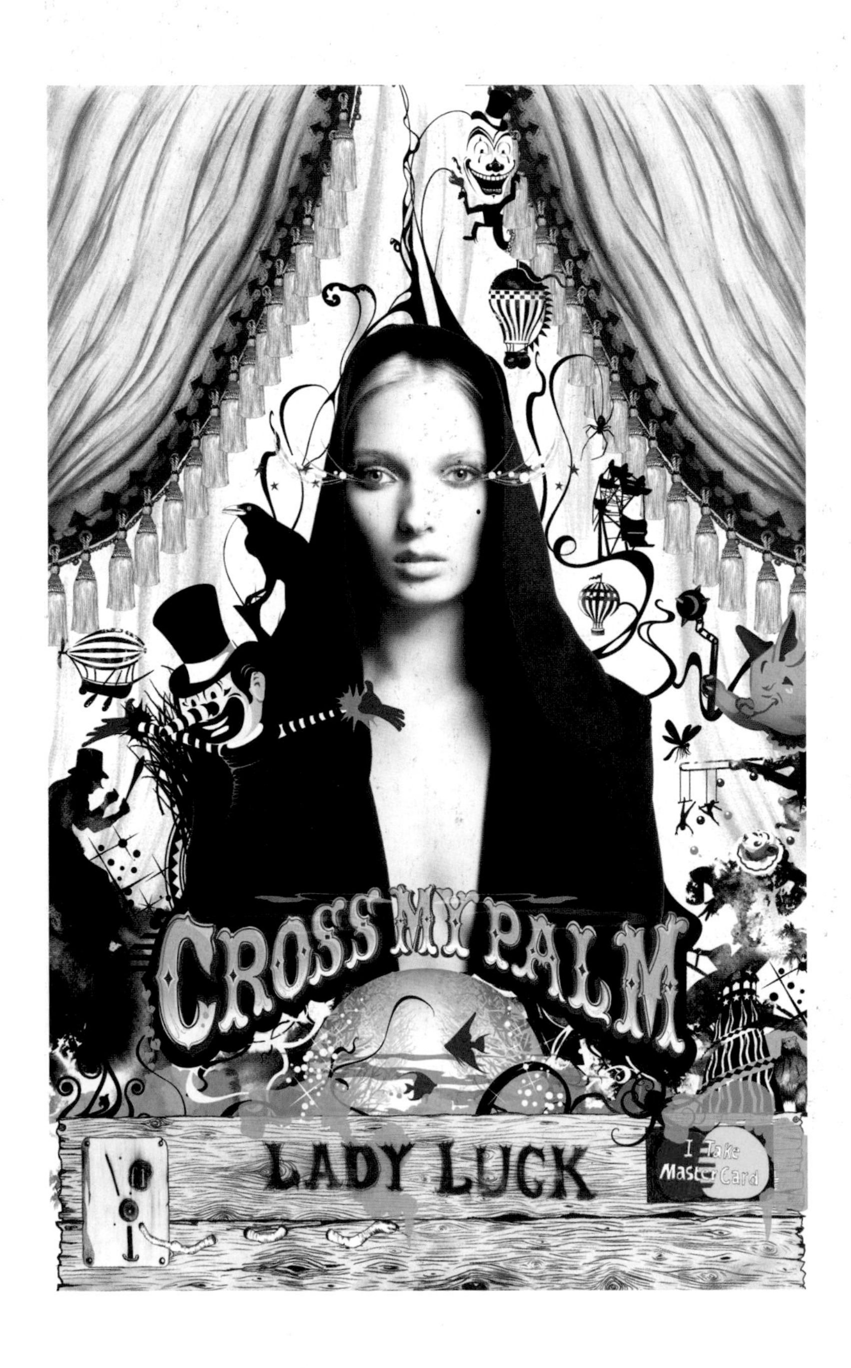

New York, USA

Title: The Greatest Show On Earth Designer: John Glasgow, Jonathan Kenyon, Daryl Waller, Si Scott Photographer: Vault49 Client: Style Montecarlo Magazine Description: The Greatest Show On Earth is inspired by a world of questionable morality and alternative pastimes, influenced by the lives and performances of early twentieth century traveling entertainers. Worlds collide to give birth to a fresh collection of unforgettable images ranging from the sublime to the fanciful.

With advance fashion collections from various designers and props from around the world, this shoot is in-keeping with the collaborative spirit in which Vault49 was conceived, The Greatest Show On Earth showcases Vault49's partnership with some of the hottest photographic, illustrative and typographic talent around.

Underwerket

Copenhagen K, Denmark

Title: - Designer: Lisa Grue Client: Underwerket
Description: Underwerket does different kind of illustrations. It is very important for Underwerket to experiment with different kind of styles, from computer illustration, to hand drawn crayon illustration, to watercolour or acrylic paintings. It is important for their creativity to be challenged in different techniques. So Underwerket loves to experiment, and not only stay in just one style the whole life. These illustrations are made for self promotion on Underwerket website. The illustration is made with crayon, ink, watercolour and mixed in the computer in photohop.

**

Maren Esdar (Unit CMA)

Amsterdam, The Netherlands

* Title: 'blossom girl' Designer: Maren Esdar
Client: Vorn, Printkultur GbR

** Title: 'ornament girl' Designer: Maren Esdar
Client: Vorn, Printkultur GbR

Description: 'blossom girl' and 'ornament girl' were created as part of a whole spread shown in combination with artworks by Edith Kollath. The main theme of the spread was about romanticism and dreaminess. The designer used a plain, white background in order not to deflect from the figures - their grace and mood. These two pieces of work have gotten a very special atmosphere, and they are one of the designer's 'all-times-favorites.'

Maren Esdar (Unit CMA)

Amsterdam, The Netherlands

* Title: 'Antwerp Fashion 2' Designer: Maren Esdar Client: Home Made Gmbh Description: The illustration was made as an opening for a city-feature about Antwerp, which is the fashion capital of Belgium and one of the most important fashion capitals of the world. The silhouette shows the roofs of Antwerp, while the figure is made up of tear-outs, showing parts of the Antwerp's fashion catwalk collections 2006. The designer also chose some sewing-attributes like scissor, in order to add some of the spirit of the fashion-ateliers and their 'work in progress' manner.

** Title: 'Girl with butterflies' Designer: Maren Esdar Client: Thames&Hudson Description: Image created exclusively Thames&Hudson's 'fashion illustration next' by Laird Borrelli.

*

**

**

*

Maren Esdar (Unit CMA)

Amsterdam, The Netherlands

* Title: 'Into the Woods' Designer: Maren Esdar Photographer: Joachim Baldauf Client: Sepp Magazine, Germany Description: It was created as an opener to the fashion spread 'ethnology' showing the latest trends of 'trapper-clothing'. In order to create an atmosphere of archaic wilderness and hunting, the designer used tear-outs from anything reminding her of wood and wilderness.

** Title: 'Flawstory' Designer: Maren Esdar Client: New York Times Description: 'Flawstory' is an illustration accompanying an article ('The Kvetchettes' by Zahra Crawford) describing the problems even the most beautiful women in the world are facing in order to get along with their physical imperfections, even though they look perfect for the masses. The designer put the face together from Angelina Jolie and Tyra Banks, because though they are incredible, beautiful women, they've gotten some extreme features.

*

**

Maren Esdar (Unit CMA)

Amsterdam, The Netherlands

* Title: 'Death' Designer: Maren Esdar Client: Attitude magazine/Remnant Media, London, UK

** Title: 'The Moon' Designer: Maren Esdar Client: Attitude magazine/Remnant Media, London, UK

Description: The image 'Death' is one out of a series of 5 tarot-cards meant to illustrate the feature 'Flirting with Disaster'.It discusses the risks that gay men may choose to put themselves in when having sex/pursuing relationships. Besides 'Death', there are the Tarot-cards 'The Moon', 'The Wheel of Fortune', 'The Tower' and 'The Lovers', all illustrated in a way related to the subject matter of the feature. 'Death' shows a young, attractive man behaving like an exhibitionist. But instead of showing his sex, he is presenting some frightful scythes to the spectator. Combined with the shine-through of his bones, he is a symbol for death.

***

****

*** Title: 'Amidala with laser-sword' Designer: Maren Esdar Client: Cream Magazine, Media Nature Limited, Hong Kong Description: 'Amidala with laser-sword' is part of a 4-pages spread about the Star Wars movies and its myths. Esdar focused on princess Amidala. The designer tried to create an atmosphere just as known from the Star Wars-movies, but giving it a very silent, concentrated mood, but still very powerful - just like in meditation.

**** Title: 'Winner' Designer: Maren Esdar Client: artmiks image builders (Dutch design agency) Description: The 'Winner' is the images created exclusively for the invitation card of the annual's contest of the Art Director's Club of the Netherlands, 2006. Esdar chose lots of glowing and rich metal tones such as gold and silver, in order to let the winner looks proud and posh, and being aware of the status.

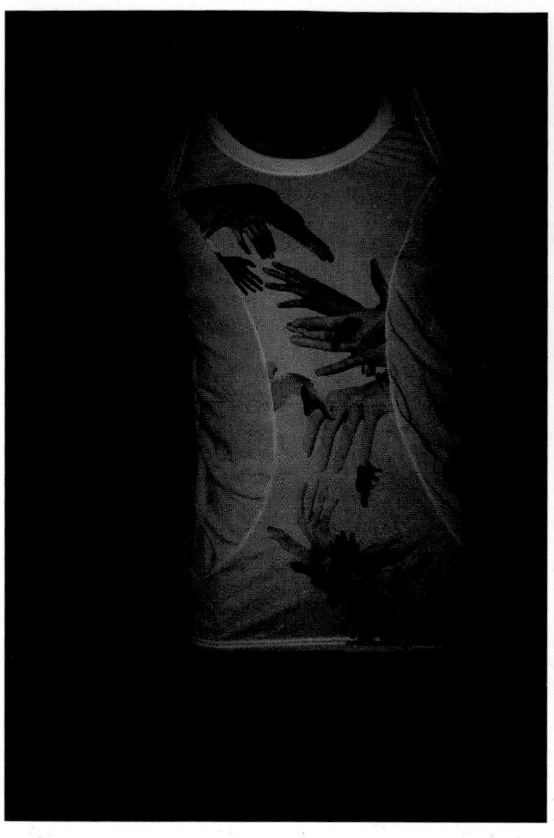

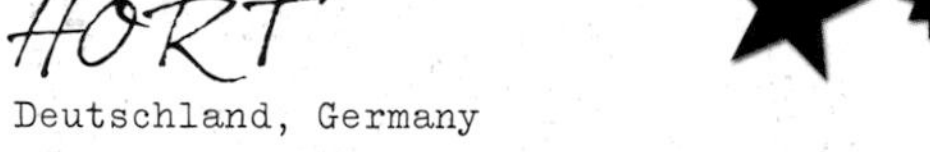

Deutschland, Germany

Title: AND A SPRING/SUMMER COLLECTION
2006 Designer: HORT Client: AND A, JAPAN
Description: -

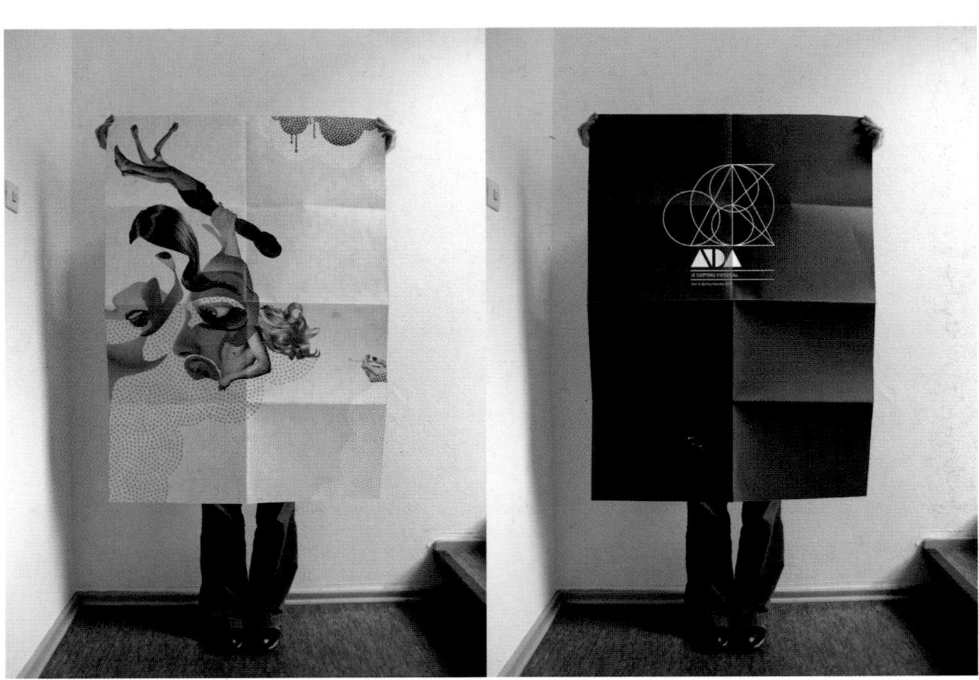
ADA
IS GETTING PHYSICAL

ADA
IS GETTING PHYSICAL

Tank Theory
New York USA

* Title: Dungeons Belt Buckle Designer: Zach Johnsen Client: Tank Theory Description: The Dungeons belt buckle is a little item forged in the fires of hell. It represents a new height for the belt buckle and carries that particularly sinister Tank Theory style. It is cast with 100% bronze and was a super limited item - only 25 are produced.

** Title: The Society Belt Buckle Designer: Zach Johnsen Client: Tank Theory Description: The Society belt buckle is another little gem in 100% cast bronze. This buckle commemorates Tank Theory artist series, the 'Society.' Again, it is a limited item - only 25 were ever produced.

*

*

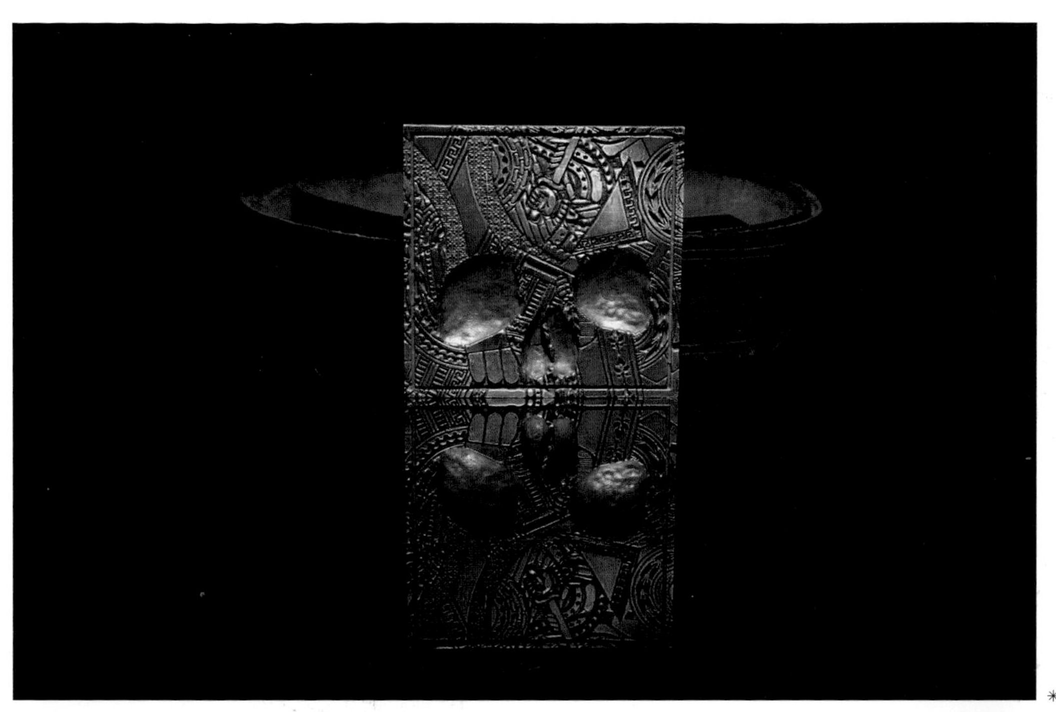

**

**

TANK THEORY
ARTIST
SOCIETY

**

Stiletto NYC

New York, USA

Title: THREEASFOUR Designer: Stiletto NYC Client: THREEASFOUR Description: Stiletto NYC has been in charge for the graphic language for a New York based fashion design collective THREEASFOUR for some years now - designing labels and clothes tags, fashion show invites, lookbooks (which turned out to be a poster in Spring/Summer 2007) and even perfume.

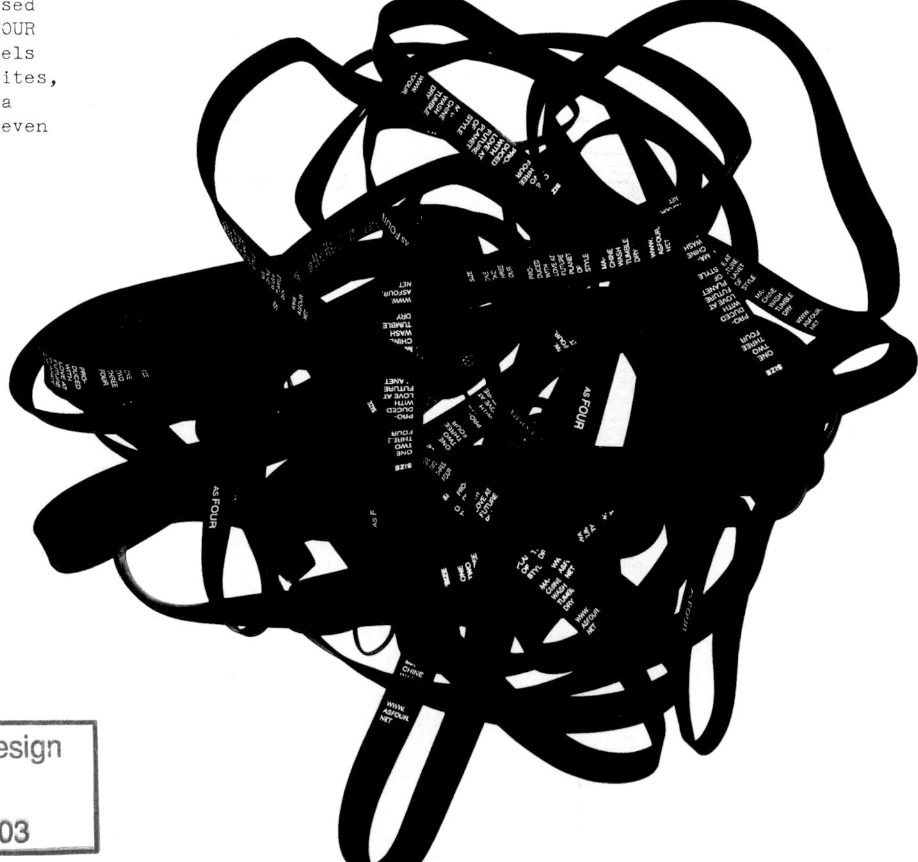

(HKI) HELLOHIKIMORI

Paris-based design studio Hellohikimori was set up in 2002 by Nathalie Melato and David Rondel Cambou. The two art directors have already been working in the design field for almost 10 years before founding the studio. Now they are working for solid and famous clients. Hellohikimori is specialized in global new media design including branding, print, web and motion design.

Page 68-69 ■

Alison Willoughby

Alison Willoughby is an established and innovative textile designer, selling and exhibiting her work both in Britain and abroad. Renowned for her highly individual and hand constructed intricate skirts, she is known as 'skirtgirl.' For Alison, a skirt is more than just a garment. It is a work of art in its own right. Made without darts, they are flat, unaffected and simple; they are the canvas on which she works, she adds structure and interest to them with three-dimensional objects such as glass spheres, hatpins and lighting filters. She experiments with various techniques: screen printing, machine and hand embroidery, and cut work with scissors to create sliced, shaved, and sculpted pieces.

Page 125 ■

Amelie Hegardt (TRAFFIC Creative Management)

Amelie studied fine art at the Stockholm School of Art, received a diploma in Art History from Stockholm University, and rounded out her studies at Central St. Martins, London. She came onto the illustration scene with a big bang in 2006 and worked extensively for several years with fringe European magazines, but had little exposure to bigger brands.

Today, being the toast of the town, Amelie's client list has quickly added MAC Cosmetics, Glamour Magazine, Black Book, Elle, Godiva Chocolates, Holt Renfrew, Bloomingdales, New York City Ballet, Umberto Giannini and Vogue Giogello Italia.

Her tightly rendered psychedelic, doodle-like, overloaded India ink and watercolour images are inspirational of the elegance of fashion silhouettes from the 1920's through to the hipster 60's psychedelic rock.

TRAFFIC Creative Management

www.trafficnyc.com

Page 222-223 ■

Anja Kroencke (TRAFFIC Creative Management)

Anja Kroencke's unusual colour combinations, texture, and spatial perception characterize her signature style. This is truly inspired by her love of architecture, furniture design and contemporary art.

After graduating in 1987 from the College for Textile & Design with a degree in Fashion Design and Illustration in Vienna, Anja pursued a career in Graphic Design and Art Direction. Anja decided to devote herself full time to her illustration career in 1997. Anja has won numerous awards and her work has appeared in American Illustration, The Art Directors Club Annuals, Society of Illustrators, Communication Arts, Print Magazine, Luerzer's Archive and The Society of Publication Designers.

In 2001 Communication Arts featured a 10-page cover story on Anja and her work. Her work was also featured in an exhibition and book called 'Fashion Illustration Now,' 2003 Thames & Hudson. In 2004 Pucci Mannequins commissioned Anja to create a line of mannequins.

TRAFFIC CREATIVE MANAGMENT

www.trafficnyc.com

Page 170-171 ■

ANREALAGE CO., LTD

DESIGNER/Kunihiko Morinaga, born in 1980 in Tokyo. Graduated from Waseda Uni as well as Vantan Career School.

Brand established in 2003. In 2005, the designer won the 'SEN-KEN h grand prix' prize in 'IFF' and 'GEN ART styles 2005, Avantgarde grand prix' prize (the contest for newcomers, held in NY). In Nov 2005, Morinaga exhibited '06 SPRING & SUMMER COLLECTION' with KEISUKE KANDA at Tokyo Tower. '06-07 AUTUMN & WINTER PRESENTATION' has exhibited with BLOCKBUSTER, clothes shaped like the 26 letters of the alphabet, based on the theme 'KANON.'

ANREALAGE's concept is 'GOD IS IN THE DETAILS,' ANREALAGE wants to reexamine ordinary lives by having a very close eye on.

Page 108-111 ■

Athletics NYC

Athletics is an art and design collective with members come together to leverage their talents and energies for a wide range of clients and projects. From publishing books and records, playing and recording music, producing and directing videos, directing independent films, and running art galleries, Athletics members have a strong commitment to creative thinking and a broad range of experience on the front lines of cultural production. Each member works both independently and together to raise the bar and to challenge clients and each other to visualize a project in a larger cultural context and to push creative possibilities.

Athletics combined client roster includes: Adidas, REM, Jimmy Eat World, Michel Gondry, Jade Tree Records, Capital Records, MTV, HBO, Sundance Channel, Sony, Leo Burnett, Ride Snowboards, 2K T-Shirts, etc.

Page 64-65 ■

Atomic Attack!

The Creative Director of Atomic Attack!, Calvin Ho studied fine art and graphic design in Sydney. 'Atomic Attack!,' a platform he started in 1997, is a multi-disciplined creative studio specializing in design, fashion, beauty, and music. He has worked on projects for like Microsoft, Sony, Nokia, Evisu, Coca Cola, Marks & Spencer, Lane Crawford, Diesel, Red Earth, Neomu USA, Hintmag.com New York and Shift.org.jp in Sapporo Japan. He is also elected as 'design news author' representing Asia for K10k.net in California since 1999. Calvin has been doing for over 12 years for parties, fashion events, with world renowned international talent such as Cassius, Dimitri, Giles Peterson, Eddie Pillar, Andy Smith, and for corporate brands Nike, Adidas, Lane Crawford, D-Mop, Diesel, Bauhaus, Nokia, IT. In 1998, he started a record shop in Hong Kong specializing in all areas of dance music and their inspirations.

Page 42-43, 179, 202-209 ■ ■ ■

■ Forest ■ Gold
■ Fuchsia ■ Black
■ Crème

Base

Formed in Brussels in 1993, Base is made up of some 45 people working from studios in Brussels, New York, Barcelona, Madrid, and Paris. The studio specializes in creative direction and brand development. As an addition to its identity work, Base in 2004 launched a writing division, BaseWORDS. In 2005, the studio added two further complementary departments: BaseMOTION, specializing in film and motion graphics, and BaseLAB, which designs custom typefaces and builds design-oriented tools. The agency also invested in Books on the Move, a comprehensive book publisher offering services in design, editorial, printing, and worldwide distribution. With a clientele that spans the corporate, cultural, and institutional sectors, Base has worked on a broad range of projects, from creating image campaigns to designing identities for major corporations and institutions.

Page 152-153, 168-169, 190, 196-199

Bleed

Working to blur the borders between graphic design, art, technology and commercial brand identity, Bleed has since its inception 6 years ago become a visible force in the world of creativity. Bleed's work spans art projects and exhibitions, identity work for several international brands as well as a book on young Nordic graphic design and running its own concept store, called One. The Oslo based outfit employs 14 people full time, representing a mix of cultures and disciplines to challenge today's conventions around art, visual language, media and identity. Bleeds seeks to add the edge, and thus to challenge the boundaries of who, what and where.

Page 226-227

Bob Foundation

Bob Foundation is established in 2002 by Mitsunori Asakura, graduated from Central St. Martins College of Art & Design BA Fine Art and Hiromi Suzuki, graduated from same college in BA Graphic Design. Bob Foundation communicates, shares and explores their interests with people through artwork, design, drawing, film, photography, text and anything else that present possibilities. They are continually dreaming, thinking and doing therefore their work is always on going.

Page 14-15, 136-137

Boredomsqueezer

Since the establishment at 2004, Boredomsqueezer has been focused on the works of graphic design and multi-media. In 2005, Boredomsqueezer has further extended their works to 3-dimensional. 'Boring Exhibition' was their first show using the action figure to present the life in Hong Kong, which came out to be very successful. By that time, Boredomsqueezer has also participated in different local and overseas exhibitions.

Page 184-185

Carmen Garcia Huerta

Huerta started as a fashion illustrator in 2001, after a short while as a graphic designer apprentice. She has been working on magazines such as ELLE, VOGUE, GLAMOUR, L'OFFICIEL, VANIDAD, EL PAIS, etc. in Spain as much as abroad. Thank to her editorial work, soon the campaigns and the branding work came along: CUSTO BARCELONA, JEAN LOUIS DAVID, CARRERA & CARRERA, ERIC BOMPARD, LOEWE, CASINOS BARRIÉRE, etc.

Page 180-183

Catalina Estrada

Born and raised in Colombia, and living in Barcelona for the past 7 years, Catalina brings all the colours and power of Latin-American folklore and refines it with a subtle touch of European sophistication. Her ability for creating fascinating illusive worlds, full of colours, nature, and enchanting characters, bursts in all of her works: art, graphic design and illustration. Presented as a fresh and new design talent by Communication Arts and Computer Arts magazines, her work has also been featured by Die Gestalten Verlag, Graphic, Swindle, IDN and DPI Magazine.

Page 22-29

COLAB eyewear

Pioneering a new movement in fashion, eyewear manufacturer, Colab is collaborating with the most talented artists around the globe. Colab's Spring/Summer 2007 collection features works by Perks & Mini, Eboy, Geoff McFetridge, Rockin' Jellybean and Neasden Control Centre. These artists morph their designs into the production of 1000 limited edition eyewear worldwide. Each pair will be individually numbered, instantly classifying them as a collectible. Artists are distinguished by colour-coded packaging. Seasonally, Colab eyewear will invite new individuals and groups to create a range that merges their own personal artistic mentality into eyewear.

Page 134-135

Commando Group

Commando Group is a graphic design and illustration agency based in Oslo, Norway. It was established in 2002 by four former colleagues with backgrounds in graphic design and illustration. Today, Commando Group is a well renowned agency specializing in advertising illustration and brand identity. The group aims to merge their skills and knowledge into solutions that help products and companies stand out as esthetic, distinctive and unique.

Page 158-159, 186-187

Deanne Cheuk Design

Deanne Cheuk is a New York based art director, illustrator and artist. She has art directed or designed many magazines, including most recently Tokion Magazine. Cheuk's art direction has been heavily influenced by her illustrative work and she is renowned for her illustrative typography. She has been commissioned by such companies as Target, Nike, Converse and MTV2 and she is a contributor to Nippon Vogue, Dazed and Confused, The Fader, The Guardian and The New York Times Magazine. Cheuk self-publishes a contributor bases graphic 'zine called 'Neomu.' Her monograph is called 'Mushroom Girls Virus.'

Page 50-51, 98-99, 172-175

DEMO

DEMO was founded by designer Justin Fines in 1997. Born out of the love of his hometown of Detroit and it's music, DEMO began by churning out flyers and ephemera for the thriving Detroit electronic music scene. Nine years, three cities, and countless projects later, Fines has found a home for DEMO in New York City. In his work, the golden tint of suburban childhood nostalgia blends with the influence of the hulking abandoned factories and mansions of the Motor City. This combination creates a graphic language that balances between hope and cynicism. Fines' work has been featured in publications worldwide, and recent projects include a toy for Superdeux & RedMagic (Hong Kong), an artist series board for Zoo York, and a series of designs for the Truth Campaign.

Page 66-67 ■

Dzark Designbureau

Dzark Designbureau is a collective of two designers based out of New York City, Virgilio Santos and Nedjelco-Michel Karlovich.

Page 210-211 ■

Edwina Hörl Japan

Edwina Hörl was born in Salzburg, Austria and autodidact as a fashion designer. Hörl had been assisted to Yohji Yamamoto from 1991-93. The designer founded the unisex label 'Edwina Hörl' in Vienna, Austria in 1996, and has been lived and worked in Tokyo, Japan since 2000. It launches twice yearly collections on a certain theme. The designer has had various presentations and exhibitions in Tokyo, Osaka, Paris, Vienna, Berlin and Sarajevo since 1996, and has worked on projects with various artists, graphic designers, architects, musicians and on theatre projects.

Page 33, 122-124 ■ ■

Erik Verdonck

Erik Verdonck graduated in 1993 at the fashion department of the Royal Academy of Fine Arts in Antwerp. He avoids the image of a regular designer by putting his freedom as creative person in the first place and commercial motivations in the second. He shows his reactions against mass production and what he calls the increasing loss of identity in the form of an annual event or presentation, the so called 'buy-buy fashion' statements. His collection, consisting exclusive handmade pieces for men and women, are mostly inspired by textile techniques, ethnical themes or fabrics and can be bought on occasional sales. He opened his own French fries shop in Antwerp. Since 2002 he designs exclusive pieces who can easily be recognized by the label inside mentioning 'size: who cares.' In this concept seasons or sizes are irrelevant.

Page 126-127 ■

Fedoralime AMFC

Founded by Michael Boyd in 2004, Fedoralime AMFC is a creative media and production boutique focusing on Creative Consultation, Art Direction, Film & Video Production, Music Production, and Website Development. It utilizes their creative and strategic network to expand and contract in size and resources unique to each client, partner, or project. The project defines the process not the other way around. What the boutique offers is a fresh and unique viewpoint on the creative process: one motivated more by the raw inspiration and individuality of message spawned from an artistic community rather than that of traditional creative agencies and strategic consultants.

Page 100-101, 188-189 ■ ■

Filip Pagowski

A New York based graphic artist, Filip Pagowski studied painting, illustration and poster design (under professor Henryk Tomaszewski) at the Warsaw Academy of Fine Arts. He works for a multitude of clients in the US, Canada, France, Japan and Poland, including The New Yorker, Comme des Garçons, Talk magazine, Saks 5th Avenue, Le Monde, Travel Leisure, The New York Times, Visionaire, Random House, Diane von Furstenberg, etc.

Page 128-133 ■

Gi Myao

Gi Myao graduated from Central St. Martins College, London. Myao is drawn to the idea of her illustrations being playful, desirable and always has a fantasy concept behind it.

Page 36-37 ■

Green Studio

Green studio was established at 2000 by Hei, now is a company with 2 creative persons named Hei and Beardsley both obtained Degree(BA) in Hong Kong Polytechnic University. Hei's profession is photography while Beardsley's is illustration and graphic design. Clients included several 4As agencies such as JWT, O&M, Leo Burnett, BBDO, Bates, Euro, Maccann, Publicis, All Right Reserved and many more.

Page 212-215, 228-229 ■

HARRIMANSTEEL

HARRIMANSTEEL was found in 1999 by Julian Harriman-Dickinson and Nick Steel, following their respective careers in advertising and design. The ethos of the designers has always been to run a broad creative agency which fully integrated to cover advertising creative through below the line activity, retail, branding, digital and graphic design work.

It is creatively led as an agency because the designers believe that the only real way to gain a connection with someone is through the spark of a really great idea. However, they also believe that design for design's sake is of little value to anyone, so all their projects are underpinned by an idea and a core desire to understand exactly what the brand is hoping to achieve.

Page 62-63 ■

Henrik Vibskov

Henrik Vibskov graduated from Central St. Martins in London and has for several years been creative in visual arts, film and music. Vibskov has been running the fashion label Henrik Vibskov since 2001 from his base in Copenhagen.

The style of Henrik Vibskov is questioning existing shapes with great reference to traditional tailoring. Adding new shapes in innovative colour combinations has captured the European (fashion) scene as well as the Japanese and worldwide market. The label is sold only in selected stores around the globe like Pineal Eye London, Mads Nørgaard Copenhagen, Midwest Tokyo, Aloharag Hawaii, Best Shop Berlin, Shine Hong Kong etc.

Henrik Vibskov has not only worked in fashion but also in plastic arts. Exhibitions have been done at Midwest Tokyo, Factory Tokyo, Millbank Gallery London, ICA London, Sotheby Gallery

New york, Palais de Tokyo Paris, vl Gallery Copenhagen, Kunstraum Kreuzberg Berlin, Hyères Festival France etc.

Page 146-151 ■

HMKM

Since the formation in 1990, HMKM has become an award winning, internationally recognized design and architecture consultancy.

HMKM has a multidisciplinary structure and teams work together to ensure all aspects of delivery are on-brand, bringing a richness of thought and originality to each project. They constantly review their skill base and approach to projects to ensure HMKM maximizes the full potential of the project brief for clients The ability to address each project holistically means that HMKM can offer an unparalleled level of service to clients and retain HMKM's position as one of the country's leading retail design consultancies.

Page 154-157 ■

HORT

HORT works on art direction and graphic design for culture, fashion, music, magazines and everything that connected with.

Page 74-85, 242-245 ■ ■

Incubate

Fortunately, much is known about Incubate's founders Dylan Nelson and Brian Acevedo. Both lived among the critters and beasts of the wild west. Nelson, an Oregon native, and Acevedo, a California dreamer, found common ground at Oregon State University. Years later, they found themselves together again in graduate school at Cranbrook Academy of Art and have since collaborated on numerous art and design related projects. They have worked with numerous clients such as Nike, Trek, Adidas, Apple, Ford, Nau amongst many others. They have also won numerous awards both nationally and internationally.

Page 18-21 ■

Ipsum Planet

Ipsum Planet is a studio of creative directors, graphic designers, copy-writers and art directors. It was founded in 1994 by Javier Abio, Ruben Manrique and Ramón Fano. Ipsum Planet works for different companies, most of them linked with fashion and art. The studio also published Neo2 magazine, with 2 editions for Spain and Portugal.

Ipsum Planet's work has been showed in different international events and museums: Arco, Palais de Tokyo, Art Futura, Sonar, Observatori, etc.

Page 102-103 ■

James Dignan (Unit CMA & Art Liaison)

James Dignan was born in New Zealand, studied fashion design & illustration at Studio Bercot in Paris, where he lived from 1985 until 2002. He has been working as a freelance illustrator for fashion, magazines, book publishing & advertising internationally since 1988. He is currently living in Sydney, Australia.

Clients include: Printemps, Galleries Lafayette, Absolut Vodka, Elizabeth Arden, Chloe, Katharine Hamnett, Escada, Hugo Boss, etc.

Magazines Include: Vogue (Australia, Singapore), Màdame Figaro (worldwide), Elle (world wide), Marie Claire (worldwide), etc.

Page 224-225 ■

Johan Hjerpe

Johan Hjerpe graduated from Beckmans College of Design in 2003. He went on to assist the artist duo Bigert & Bergstrom whilst studying Contemporary Aesthetics. It was during this time that he started his live illustration performance act Mistermusic at various clubs and galleries. Johan then was granted a joint production and exhibition space at the art institution Konst2 where he developed an interest in communication strategies. Soon he began working for global clients such as Iittala, Bang & Olufsen and Electrolux through the brand development agency Grow.

After a period as graphic designer for the Royal Dramatic Theatre in Stockholm, Johan Hjerpe now runs his own studio. His work builds a language of elements that play with cultural codes and meaning, where every detail, whether colour, shape or form, is a prop in a larger ongoing narrative.

Page 35, 178, 218-219 ■ ■ ■

kidnapyourdesigner

kidnapyourdesigner is a Belgian graphic studio, created by Caroline Dath graduated from Saint-Luc Liège (Belgium) and from ERG (Graphic School of Research in Brussels). The studio, based in Brussels, capital of Europe, produces graphic identities, printing works, edition and also some experimental video projects standing at the crossroads of European influences (Netherlands, England, Switzerland).

www.kidnapyourdesinger.com

Page 138-139 ■

Kinetic Design & Advertising, Singapore

Kinetic Singapore is an award-winning design & advertising agency based in Singapore. Established in 2001, the agency has since worked with many high profile global brands including Nokia, Nike and Citibank. To date, it has garnered recognition from major international awards and has been featured in various design publications and magazines.

Page 86-87 ■

Krv Kurva Design

Created in 2003 as a join venture by Jorge Moita and Daniela Pais, Krv Kurva Design has been acting as R&D Studio, for the fashion and design industry. 'May we dress anything?' is the main question. The start up point was the project of La.Ga Bag, developed and produced by the two designers. La.Ga has been produced since then and is worldwide distributed with a cultural representation trough 'To Love Is Not An Option'. Krv Kurva acts and reacts with several clients from public institutions to friends and from international 'thinkers' to boring neighbours. Based in Lisbon the Krv Kurva team has just moved from Real Kitchen studio, their ex-lab to Krv Kurva. 09o 08` 34.51``W, 28o 42` 12.65``N The new spot.

Page 114-115 ■

Kustaa Saksi (Unit CMA)

Kustaa Saksi's illustrations are a syrupy disarray of elements: playful, paradoxical, often over-glossy, inviting, troubling, messy, and yet strangely clear. Finnish-born illustrator, nowadays living and working in Paris, combines organic touches and viscous shapes into new world pyschedelia. Saksi has been working with various clients in the world of fashion, music and entertainment. He's unique imagination with strict Scandinavian design roots illustrates the wonderful world of surrealistic landscapes, beautifully strange characters and very strong atmosphere.

Page 34, 38-39 ■

Made

Made is a multi-disciplinary design studio based in Oslo, Norway. They can be found far up in the mountains, in the middle of the fjords or deep in the forest. Made was established in 2004/2005 by three partners, and constantly grows. Made works with a diverse range of projects, and believe in the strength of a good idea. The client list is impressive, diverse and so is the work produced. Made is part of the worldwide TBWA group.

Page 104, 140-141 ■ ■

Maren Esdar (Unit CMA)

Maren Esdar was educated both as a stylist and illustrator in Hamburg (University of Applied Sciences) and London (Central St. Martins). Her extravagantly, surreal and stylishly collages were published in the world's most influential fashion and style magazines, i.a. Vogue,*Surface, New York Times Magazine. Her work has been featured in stunning book-projects such as Laird Borrelli's 'Fashion Illustration Next'/Thames&Hudson, 'Wonderland,' 'Designed to Help,' 'illusive' and 'all allure'/Die Gestalten Verlag, which focused on the most innovative and exciting of the newly established names and a host of stars in the making. She lives and works in Hamburg and N.Y.C where she also co-owns an art-agency called style_unique.

Page 236-241 ■

MATERIALBYPRODUCT

The studio MATERIALBYPRODUCT is so named because designers Susan Dimasi & Chantal McDonald see themselves as the designers of systems rather than things, hence the fashion materialized is the by-product of these systems. At the core of the studio exists a workroom where there is a high value placed in craftsmanship and the building of an innovative house. The collaboration is hinged around a common investigation of tailoring and drapery with traditional processes intersected by conscious departures from the one which has become habitual to produce numerous different outcomes and innovate mastery.

Page 191-195 ■

MIXKO

MIXKO is a design partnership formed by Goldsmiths College graduates Nahoko Koyama and Alex Garnett. Both had their work selected by the British Council during Milan Furniture Fair 2003, and featured in influential magazines whilst undergraduates. Since then they have continued to earn critical acclaim for their creations at various international design events.

MIXKO's aim is to create items that have a wide appeal, inspire happiness and possess a satisfying simplicity. Nahoko and Alex are continually seeking fresh design ideas to meet various everyday needs with original thinking.

Page 30-32 ■

Nam Kong

Nam Kong is the founder of 'Store' Magazine, and took up the post of Publisher and Editorial & Creative Director during 2002 - 2003. Kong obtained Degree(BA) in Hong Kong Polytechnic University with the major in Photography. He has been working on the editorial for many Hong Kong fashion magazines, photography, writing and art direction. Kong is the Creative Director of the production studio store n*2. He participates in styling of many local pop stars, and the advertising shooting of various fashion brands. In June 2003, his photographic and art direction work was exhibited in the 'Home Design Exhibition' in the Hong Kong Polytechnic University. The designer was invited to participate in the 'HELLO KITTY hide & seek Exhibition.'

Page 105-107 ■

NoPattern

Chuck Anderson is an artist/designer from the Chicago area. He has been freelancing since 2004 when he was 18. He has worked with Island/Def Jam, Reebok, Sony, Nike and more. Aside from his commercial work, he runs www.nopattern.com and www.npandco.com, his portfolio site and online store, respectively. In addition to his work, he also speaks at events and universities and judges several prestigious awards and competitions including the 2006 Art Director's Club Awards.

Page 60-61 ■

outasight Co., Ltd.

Hal Yamagiwa worked at Song Music Design Department in 2000. In the year 2002, he studied at the Sandberg Institute (Postgraduate Design Academy) in Amsterdam, the Netherlands. A year later, he launched the design company 'outasight Co., Ltd.' and started the fashion brand 'sureshot' in 2004. He is currently managing 2 fashion brands ('sureshot' & 'outasight'), graphic design, illustrations and various art projects.

Page 96-97 ■

Plazm Media, Inc.

Founded in 1991 by artists as a creative resource, Plazm publishes an eclectic design and culture magazine with worldwide distribution and operates an innovative type foundry. Plazm is also a design firm that builds identities, advertising, interactive and retail experiences using custom typography. Plazm authored the book XXX: The Power of Sex in Contemporary Design, and is working on a new series of books about creative expression on the margins of culture. Current projects include a Plazm monograph, a twenty-plus variation customized global type identity for Nike and a new magazine launch for Adobe.

Page 88-91, 164-165 ■ ■

potipoti Graphic Fashion

potipoti is a graphic fashion company founded in Berlin by two Spanish illustrators and designers: Silvia Salvador and Nando Cornejo.

Nando&Silvia have kept themselves busy all this time joining their talents in animation, illustration, graphic and fashion design as well as doing gallery exhibitions and visual arts for dif-

ferent clubs. potipoti's image is inspired in a fantastic world of geometric and simple trace creatures which have both naive and sinister souls. A mixture of rage and tenderness.

Page 9-13, 142-145 ■ ■

Rebecca Wetzler

Rebecca Wetzler was born in 1982 in Northampton Massachusetts USA. Grew up in Perth where she graduated from West Australian School of Art & Design, then went onto get a BA in Design (Illustration) at Curtin University in 2004. Wetzler now resides in Sydney, with her studio located in Surry Hills. Working with Designer's such as Mimco and Vicious Threads. Wetzler's work has been published in magazines such as Oyster, Marie Claire, Yen and Deanne Cheuk's ongoing illustration project Neomu.

Page 216-217 ■

Sara Hernández

Born in Stockholm 1976, Sara Hernández was grown up in south of Stockholm. After college Sara studied fine art, exploring her interest in drawing and sculpture. After a year working as a studio assistant, first at a children book publisher and later at a design studio, her struggling work finally had a breakthrough when she had the opportunity to study graphic design at Beckmans School of design 2000-2003. Since graduation she has been working with illustration and graphic design on freelance basis. She does a lot of illustration and often uses photographs both as reference and inspiration. Graphic black and white style but lately she has started to use more colour. Sara's aim is to continue work within the fashion scene as an illustrator and designer.

Page 44-45 ■

Sara Lamúrias Unipessoal Lda (aforest-design)

A forest is a brand for passion, for small and big life events. Artists, dreamers, politically or socially aware or not. Young ones, no matter what age. aforest-design launches products and collections with strong ideas, some of them in limited editions or on order. Wear to think.

Page 112-113, 120-121 ■

Saturday London

Saturday as an idea was born somewhere 30,000 feet over the Black Sea, on the way to attend the opening of Villa Moda, a one-of-a-kind luxury retail emporium in Kuwait, of which Erik Torstensson and Jens Grede - Saturday's two Swedish co-founders - had overseen the creative direction. Their idea was to create an agency for clients who believe that aspirational advertising and design are a commercial advantage regardless of a brand's price point. Now more than 4 years later, Saturday has fulfilled its promise and works with image-conscious clients all over the world: Among them H&M, Swarovski, Boots and Kurt Geiger. To name a few, London has provided the perfect base for the young agency that since its incarnation, has grown into a full service creative agency that can handle size of project.

Page 72-73, 94-95, 166-167, 200 ■ ■

Scandinavian DesignLab

'Despite extensive design experience - you must always consider yourself being green!'

At Scandinavian DesignLab the award winning designers often kill their darlings and seeks new solutions. The aim is creating innovative graphic design - and the means are freedom to play, hunger for pushing the limits and big hearts beating for new challenging creative ideas within corporate identity, brand building, packaging design and fashion.

Page 160-163 ■

Serial Cut™

Serial Cut™ is a Madrid based studio, established in 1999 by Sergio del Puerto, licensed in Visual Communication in the UCM (Madrid) and graphic design, working on great variety of projects types although mainly focus on Art Direction, Design & Illustration.

Serial Cut™ works with national and international clients. Some of them are: Nike (USA), WAD Magazine (France), Details Magazine (USA), Rolling Stone, MTV Magazine, Istituto Europeo di Design, TWBA, Publicis, McCann, Lucky Strike, Clone, Urbana Recordings, Editorial Salto de Página, EME Estilistas, LeChic.

Page 40-41, 70-71 ■ ■

Serum Vs Venom / SVSV

SVSV is a modern design brand based on Future Craft, a design philosophy that explores the collisions between craftsmanship, advanced technology, extreme individualism and utility. SVSV ultimately believes that less is truly more. SVSV products are designed, produced and sold exclusively through their private New York Showroom & Workshop. They strongly believe that in today's over-saturated world, the direct relationship between designers and customers is one of the last realms of true value.

Page 201 ■

Shya-la-la Production Limited

Shya-La-La is an independent visual communications agency that offers a one-stop integrated communication from visual design to advertising, product design to packaging, corporate identity to collaterals, photography to multimedia, character design to illustration and content licensing. Shya-La-La believes that projects with a wholesome concept and is artistically presented will have a lasting impression in the mind of the consumers. Their objective is to create the bridge through the marketing process, and their vision is to speak to client's consumers via their creations.

Page 54-56 ■

Something and Something Else

SOMETHING is a brand that chooses to define street fashion by not really defining it. The core of Something consists of creator Natalie Wood, and a talented group of artists that help to create the clever and intricate print work that defines Something. A/W 2006 saw the introduction of SOMETHING ELSE, the newest installment from Natalie and her friends. The collection is an artful and experimental collaboration which continues to push the boundaries further than SOMETHING, and offers up a broad array of beautiful and clever graphics fused with directional styling.

Page 46-49, 52-53 ■

Staple Design

With an impressive client roster that includes Burton Snowboards,

Levi's, LVMH, New Balance, Nike, Original Penguin, Polo, Puma, Timberland, Uniqlo, Zoo York, The Fader Magazine, Apple Computer and Sony Playstation; Staple Design has done everything from creating one of the most highly coveted sneakers in history, to complete brand identity and related collateral for other world-class companies. Staple Design also creates an in-house, eponymous fashion label which is sold in top boutiques all over the globe. In 2002, Staple Design opened Reed Space which is a retail store and art gallery committed to placing the spotlight on the creative process. It features art, fashion, books, music and magazines.

Page 92-93 ■

Stiletto NYC

Stiletto NYC is a design studio based in New York & Milan, that specializes in art direction & design for print and video. It was co-founded in 2000 by Stefanie Barth and Julie Hirschfeld. Stiletto works with such clients as MTV, Nike, CondeNast, HBO, HKM films, architect Andrea Tognon, the New York fashion collective Threeasfour and several boutiques & individuals in Europe and America. Stiletto has been featured in publications internationally and spoke at Semi-permanent design conference in Sydney Australia in 2006.

Page 248 ■

Studio I'm JAC

The designer studied Fashion Illustration at St. Joost art academie, in Breda The Netherlands. Studio I'm JAC works freelance for advertising agencies, magazines and books. Located in Rotterdam the Netherlands.

Page 16-17 ■

Studio Job

Studio Job designs projects in arts, design, architecture and fashion. Based in Belgium and The Netherlands, Studio Job works with international companies as Bulgari, Bisazza, Swarovski and design labels like Viktor & Rolf. Galleries where objects and products of Studio Job are sold are: eg Moss in New York, Dilmos in Milan, Cibone in Tokyo.

Page 116-117 ■

Surface to air. Paris

Born in Paris in 2000, SURFACE TO AIR Paris is a creative studio/boutique operating in art, fashion and communication. The designers' need for freedom and independence, conditions to creativity, made them organize themselves around high pluri-disciplinary activities and projects in the creative domains which interest them. In total there are 14 people of different origins and backgrounds based in Paris. The group consists of: SURFACE TO AIR STUDIO / S2A STUDIO (est.2001), SURFACE TO AIR MEN PARIS collection (est.2004) and RENDEZ-VOUS (est.2003).

Page 118-119, 176-177 ■ ■

Tank Theory

Uncovered from the dusty cellars and attics of cornfield farmhouses and military issue ammunition boxes. Original in concept, design and execution.

Page 246-247 ■

Toby Neilan

After studying at Chelsea School of Art and Middlesex University Neilan specialized in printmaking. As a printmaker lacking studio space the designer began using the computer, digitally manipulating his photographs, combining drawing and mark making and upholding the aesthetics of printmaking. Neilan's artwork falls into two main categories, Architecture and Fashion. The latter being a collaboration with make-up artist Sharon Dowsett, documenting backstage at Fashion Week in London, Milan and Paris.

Clients include Issey Miyake, Y-3, IBM and MTV and for editorial Blueprint, Mark, Tank, Commons and Sense and Mixte.

Page 58-59 ■

Underwerket

Underwerket works in the field of cross over between art and design. Co-founder Lisa Grue has carved quite a name for herself and her studio Underwerket with her fine art work, illustrating and doing conceptual design for books, fashion and design magazines, as well as fashion labels.

Lisa Grue/Underwerket has garnered applause with her sublime cocktail of - in your -face attitude, and poetic femininity. Lisa and her studio Underwerket is an especially active personality in the Danish art/design environment, appearing in several exhibitions in Denmark and Europe. Lisa has been honored with several grants from the National Art foundation of Denmark.

Page 234-235 ■

Vault49 LLC

Graduating together from the London College of Printing, Jonathan Kenyon and John Glasgow launched Vault49 alongside their final year degree show. The collaboration quickly emerged as one of the UK's leading and most innovative design companies with a broad portfolio spanning typography, illustration, photography and animation.

Following their relocation to New York in 2004, Vault49 continues to achieve sustained coverage in the best of the UK, US and worldwide design press by virtue of the breathe of their ability across all fields of design, and reputation for creating consistently innovative work for an international client list.

Page 230-233 ■

why not associates

why not associates is a british graphic design company with global reach. They turn their passion for design into commercial success for clients in business, government and the public sector. For nearly two decades, why not associates has been creating innovative work for clients large and small. The team works in many different media on many types of projects, including corporate identity, digital design, motion graphics and television commercial direction, editorial design, environmental design, publishing, and public art.

Page 57 ■

Yke Schotten (Unit CMA)

Yke Schotten, artist and illustrator, lives and works in Rotterdam, the Netherlands. Represented by Unit Creative Management Amsterdam, the Netherlands.

Page 220-221 ■

Acknowledgements

We would like to thank all the designers and companies who made a significant contribution to the compilation of this book. Without them, this project would not have been possible.

We would like to thank Kustaa Saksi for the cover illustration and all the producers for their invaluable assistance throughout. Its successful completion also owes a great deal to many professionals in the creative industry who have given us precious insights and comments. We are also very grateful to many other people whose names do not appear on the credits for making specific input and continuous support the whole time.

Viction:ary

Future Editions

If you would like to contribute to the next edition of Victionary, please email us your details to submit@victionary.com